RMS
TITANIC

1909–12 (Olympic Class)

First published in April 2011
Reprinted January 2012, April 2014

A catalogue record for this book is available from the
British Library

ISBN 978 1 84425 662 4

Library of Congress control no. 2010937159

Published by Haynes Publishing,
Sparkford, Yeovil, Somerset BA22 7JJ, UK
Tel: 01963 442030 Fax: 01963 440001
Int. tel: +44 1963 442030 Int. fax: +44 1963 440001
E-mail: sales@haynes.co.uk
Website: www.haynes.co.uk

Haynes North America Inc.
861 Lawrence Drive, Newbury Park,
California 91320, USA

**While every effort is taken to ensure the accuracy
of the information given in this book, no liability
can be accepted by the author or publishers for
any loss, damage or injury caused by errors in, or
omissions from the information given.**

Printed in the USA by Odcombe Press LP,
1299 Bridgestone Parkway, La Vergne, TN 37086

COVER CUTAWAY:
RMS Titanic. *(John Lawson)*

RMS TITANIC

1909–12 (Olympic Class)

Owners' Workshop Manual

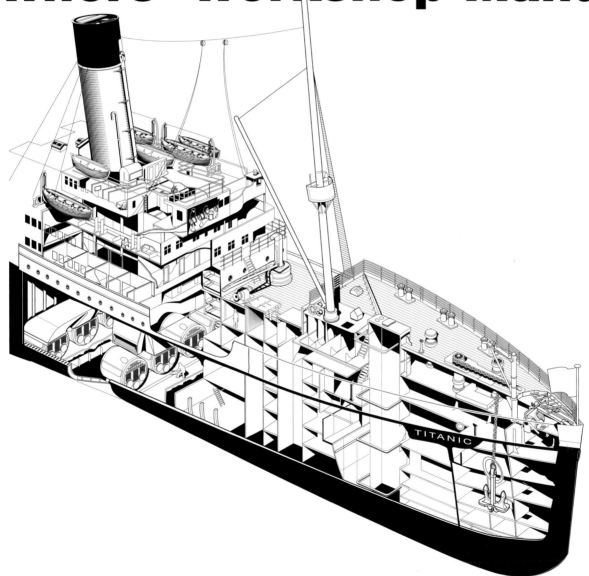

An insight into the design, construction and operation of the
most famous passenger ship of all time

David F. Hutchings and Richard de Kerbrech

Contents

OPPOSITE Women enter a lifeboat from B Deck of the *Titanic*.
Drawn from material supplied by Mr F.M. Hoyt, a survivor. *(TopFoto)*

Introduction

For more than a century the White Star liner *Titanic* has been synonymous with sheer size, unimaginable opulence and great tragedy. From the moment she was launched at Belfast in 1911, *Titanic* became a ship of superlatives. She was a seagoing wonder of the Edwardian age, and the memory of her calamitous sinking on 15 April 1912 has continued to live on in popular memory.

OPPOSITE As she began her journey down Southampton Water on 10 April 1912, the water displaced by the *Titanic* caused the mooring ropes of the liner *New York* (left) to snap. Her stern drifted out towards the *Titanic* (centre) that was passing broadside to her. A collision was only averted through the quick actions of the *Titanic*'s Captain Smith, Harbour Pilot Bowyer, and Captain Gale of the tug *Vulcan* (foreground). An hour later, the *Titanic* resumed her voyage. *(TopFoto)*

In the following pages you can read about the *Titanic*'s design and construction, the working of her massive engines, and what it took – above and below decks – to operate this 42,000-ton leviathan. Despite being at the cutting edge of early 20th century design and technology, an object as simple as an iceberg was responsible for sending the *Titanic* to the bottom of the North Atlantic on her maiden voyage.

For a manual dealing with a ship of any size, let alone one so complex, large and historic as the *Titanic*, it is not easy to gauge the depth and scope of what should be included. It has been decided, therefore, to focus on certain major aspects of description and maintenance.

Wherever possible the *Titanic*'s engineering and hull components have been described from the ship's actual technical specifications. Where these have not been known or were unavailable, technical details have been taken from contemporary marine engineering and naval architecture literature. Of necessity, because the *Titanic* was the second of a class of three ships, on occasions it has been necessary to refer to her earlier sister, the *Olympic*, and to a lesser extent to the last of the trio, the *Britannic*. Again, where technical details of the *Titanic* have been scant or have not been available, her two sister ships have been used to provide illustrations and descriptions.

Many repair and maintenance activities

LEFT The huge casing of one of the two engine change-over valves. *(The Shipbuilder)*

that might have been carried out on the *Titanic* had she survived would have been lengthy and complex, and these have been judged to be outside the scope of this manual. With this in mind, some typical repair and maintenance activities have been selected to give readers an insight into both the daily running of the ship and the more extensive maintenance that might have been undertaken when dry-docked.

Take, for example, the removal and subsequent refitting of one of the *Titanic*'s twin 38-ton wing propellers. This was a major undertaking and would have required the great ship to be dry-docked during a major maintenance period. To describe this activity in detail would take many thousands of words. Instead, a brief synopsis is presented of what might have been required – including emptying millions of gallons of water from the Thompson Graving Dock, the use of a 200-ton-lift floating crane and the erection of acres of scaffolding.

In a work of this nature the use of a range of technical terms and expressions is unavoidable. A comprehensive glossary has been included at the end of the book to help explain these to the lay person. All units of measurement are in Imperial quantities, as befitting those used in shipyards of the day; the exception is electrical power, which is quoted in watts (W) or kilowatts

(kW). Where there is reference to gross and displacement tonnages, masses and weights of machinery and bunker coal, Imperial tons have been used (made up of 2,240lb), which were known in the United States as 'long tons'.

We hope readers enjoy this insight into one of the most historic passenger liners of the 20th century.

David Hutchings, Lee-on-The Solent
Richard de Kerbrech, Isle of Wight

Acknowledgements

The authors would like to extend their gratitude to the following people, firms and institutions for their kindness in contributing information and illustrations and other help: Boat Building Academy Ltd, Lyme Regis Marine Centre (especially Yvonne Green, Principal, Emma Brice and Ian Baird); Jack Eaton; Charles Haas; Robert Hunter; Tom McCluskie; the late William McQuitty; Simon Mills; Harold Reemsnyder; David Williams; Getty Images; National Museums Northern Ireland; PA Images; Topfoto. Without their assistance this book would certainly not have been written.

To the following for their support and sharing their technical knowledge: Mark Chirnside, Samuel Halpern, David Lawrence, John Siggins, Ivan Taylor, and Alan McCartney of the Ulster Folk & Transport Museum; and finally our thanks to our commissioning editor at Haynes, Jonathan Falconer, who thought up this hare-brained idea.

Chapter One

The *Titanic* Story

Titanic – the second of the Olympic Class liners – was not revolutionary in design, but was remarkable for her size, with dimensions being extrapolated from previously proven plans. Her 15 watertight bulkheads were said at the time to make the ship 'practically unsinkable'. But, in hindsight, these bulkheads did not extend high enough, and this, along with insufficient lifeboats, proved to be her Achilles' heel.

Presenting a magnificent sight, *Titanic* is gently ushered into Belfast Lough by her attendant tugs of the Alexandra Towing Co., **2 April 1912.** *(Ulster Folk & Transport Museum – UTFM – H1721)*

Harland & Wolff's Olympic Class

The White Star Line, which began trading as a transatlantic steamship company in 1869, declared a policy of placing supreme comfort and size before speed with the introduction of the innovative *Oceanic* of 1899. This move gained the company a considerable following with the travelling public and a reputation for excellence. In 1902 the company was taken over by John Pierpont Morgan's large United States shipping combine, the International Mercantile Marine Company (IMMCo), but still traded as the White Star Line.

By 1908 an emigrant could travel to the United States for just £2 ($10) and J.P. Morgan saw fixed prices as a means of eliminating the competition. For J. Bruce Ismay, then chairman of White Star, one of the answers to the stiff competition from Cunard and other shipping companies from the Continent was to build larger and finer ships with greater carrying capacity.

So it was that one midsummer night in 1907, J. Bruce Ismay, chairman of White Star and president of IMMCo, dined at the Belgravia home of Lord Pirrie, chairman of Harland & Wolff. Lord Pirrie, who as William Pirrie had spent four years serving a 'gentleman apprenticeship' in the drawing office, learning how to design and build ships, rose through the early days at Harland & Wolff to be made a partner in 1876. After the death of Sir Edward Harland in December 1895, Pirrie was made chairman the following year. At the time of this meeting, Cunard Line's *Lusitania* had entered

service, with the *Mauretania* nearing completion. The conversation between the two men and their wives turned to ships that might be built to counter Cunard's lead. From the informal discussions came a proposal to build a class of two vessels of immense size, which would later become the *Olympic, Titanic* and a third, the *Britannic* (originally proposed as the *Gigantic*), would later be ordered. The fact that there were no slipways, dry docks or even a pier that could accommodate a ship of their proposed size would have to be overcome. These liners would make the Atlantic crossing in under a week. However, the emphasis would be on safety and comfort rather than speed, which was often accompanied by an increase in uncomfortable vibration. The comfort would be on a scale so magnificent that the few additional hours at sea on these 'floating palaces' would be savoured.

Cash would be made available because of White Star's pre-eminent position in IMMCo, and its owner, J. Pierpont Morgan, stipulated that he would underwrite 'the finest vessels afloat'. This may have been said with a little trepidation for it was White Star's first innovation of such a large class of liner on the North Atlantic since the American owners had acquired the company in 1902. For IMMCo this might well be a leap in the dark.

A fixed price contract of £3 million for the *Olympic* and *Titanic* was agreed, but this did not preclude Harland & Wolff from submitting a larger account for 'extras to contract'. A profit margin was added to the actual cost of the ship and this was known as 'cost plus basis'.

Prior to ships of the Olympic Class being constructed, new slipways had to be built and extended. In order to accommodate these large vessels, Harland & Wolff demolished three existing slipways, including one vacated by the *Laurentic* in its Queen's Island shipyard, and built two much larger ones in their place, namely slipways No. 2 and No. 3. The ground beneath the new slips was piled throughout and covered with concrete 4½ft deep. To facilitate the economical erection and hydraulic riveting of the two ships, two enormous gantries were constructed over the slips and equipped with a system of moving cranes travelling on

BELOW *Titanic during her fitting out at Harland & Wolff's Belfast shipyard.*
(Harland & Wolff)

The White Star Line

The White Star Line began as a sailing-ship concern, trading to Australia. Its name and goodwill was bought in 1867 for £1,000 by Thomas Henry Ismay, who, two years later, started to operate a purely steamship company across the Atlantic known as the Oceanic Steam Navigation Company (OSNCo), but trading under the banner of the White Star Line.

White Star's first steamship, *Oceanic*, (1871–96) was an innovative iron-hulled vessel of 3,707 gross tons, and it was with this ship that its service to North America was inaugurated. Although a comparative latecomer on the North Atlantic in 1871 with the first *Oceanic*, White Star soon established a reputation for comfort, luxury, speed and reliability. At the end of the 19th century White Star was one of the premier shipping companies in existence. Not only this, but its status was enhanced because many of the company's masters and officers held commissions in the Royal Naval Reserve (RNR), which entitled their vessels to sail under the Blue Ensign.

On the death of Thomas Ismay in November 1899 the control of the White Star Line passed to his eldest son, Joseph Bruce Ismay. The same year a second, improved, *Oceanic* entered service.

By 1902 the company had been taken over by John Pierpont Morgan's large American shipping combine, IMMCo. From this time, through the Edwardian era, it went from strength to strength until it reached its zenith with the introduction of the *Olympic* and *Titanic*. The loss of the *Titanic* in 1912 damaged the company's reputation almost beyond repair, and was followed by the First World War during which it incurred the loss of the *Olympic*'s other sister, the *Britannic*. After the war, the company bounced back with the confiscated German liners *Majestic*, *Homeric* and *Arabic*. It managed to survive the era under the Royal Mail group of companies until the Depression, only to be absorbed by its largest rival, Cunard, in 1934.

Also intertwined with White Star was Harland & Wolff of Belfast, the builder of almost every White Star vessel. It, too, prospered from White Star's reputation in a close partnership that lasted for 62 years.

The combination of financial irregularities within the Royal Mail group, the Depression and pressure to merge with its rival Cunard unwittingly conspired towards White Star's downfall and its premature demise from the North Atlantic. When White Star was absorbed by the Cunard merger of 1934 some of its liners were hastily dispatched to the breakers with the exception of three that remained in service until the Second World War. The company's livery and nomenclature passed to Shaw Savill & Albion, which for 51 years had maintained a joint service on the New Zealand route.

BELOW Advance publicity for the *Titanic*. American posters advertised her return fares from New York to Southampton. *(The Granger Collection/ Topfoto)*

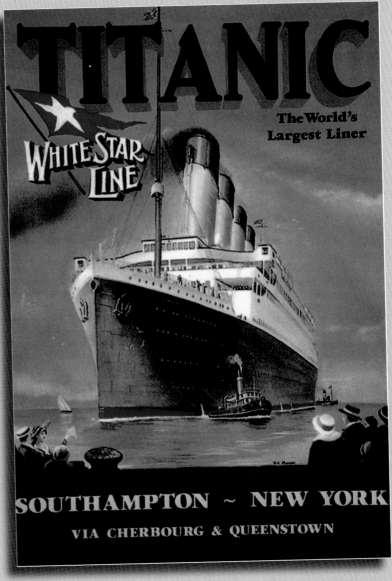

ABOVE *Olympic* (right) painted white for the cameras in readiness for her launch on 20 October 1910. *Titanic* is still under construction, and both are framed by the Arrol gantry. A steel stockyard dominates the foreground with its stacks of plating. *(UFTM WAG 2079)*

RIGHT Thomas Andrews, 39-year-old managing director of Harland & Wolff's Design Department, was the nephew of Lord Pirrie, chairman of the shipbuilding company. *(Topham Picturepoint/Press Association Images)*

overhead rails, and with four large electric lifts. The Glasgow firm of Sir William Arrol & Co Ltd erected these and they covered an area of 840ft x 240ft. The height of the travelling cranes was 214ft. In addition to modifications to the joiners' shop and others, the platers' shed was remodelled and equipped with machinery to handle the steel platework for the two liners. A 200-ton floating crane was purchased from Deutsche Maschinenfabrik AG of Duisburg in Germany to lift the propelling machinery and boilers on board during their fitting-out stage after launch.

Preparations were not confined to Harland & Wolff, for it was necessary that adequate berthing and dry-docking facilities would be available for the new vessels on their completion. In concert with Harland & Wolff, Belfast Harbour Commissioners had begun the construction of a new graving (dry) dock during 1903. Designed to be the largest in the world, it was completed in 1911 in time to permit the dry-docking of the *Olympic* on 1 April that year. Thus the foundations were laid for White Star's and Harland & Wolff's most ambitious and costliest project to date.

The Harland & Wolff team responsible for the design of the Olympic Class comprised Lord Pirrie, Thomas Andrews (the managing director of the design department), Lord Pirrie's nephew Edward Wilding (deputy to Andrews and responsible for the design calculations, stability and trim), and Alexander M. Carlisle (Harland & Wolff's chief naval architect).

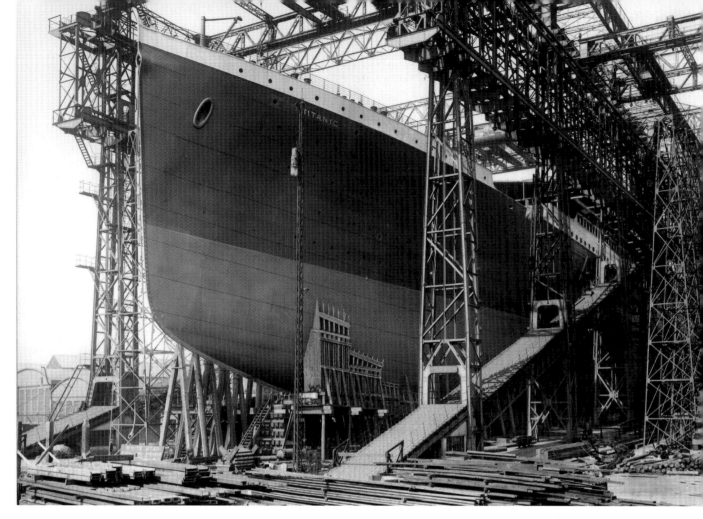

The *Titanic* is born

Although the *Olympic* was the first of the class to be laid down and built, the *Titanic*'s life began with the laying of her keel on 31 March 1909 as Yard No. 401. At the time of the construction of the *Olympic* and *Titanic*, Harland & Wolff had a workforce of around 14,000 men and at any time between 3,000 and 4,000 of these would be allocated to the building of the two sisters.

Shop managers, foremen, craftsmen, labourers and apprentices referred to detailed drawings and from these manufactured from steel, wood, copper, brass and glass the frames, plates, engines, boilers and thousands of other items that would, together, create the largest ship ever built to that date. Meticulously drawn and tinted plans were prepared for the ship's interior decor, showing panelling, classical columns, furniture, doors, window frames and the hundreds of other skilfully made items that were required to fit out a floating luxury hotel.

The *Titanic*'s huge structure rose in the gantry against the Belfast skyline. After the construction of her hull, the shafting and its supporting bearings were installed; her three propellers were fitted after her launch. The centre propeller was four-bladed, cast manganese bronze, of 16ft 6in diameter, that would be driven by the Parsons low-pressure exhaust turbine. The two outward-turning, three-bladed wing propellers built up from cast steel hubs and bolted-on bronze blades were 23ft 6in in diameter and would be driven by the *Titanic*'s steam reciprocating engines. The *Titanic*'s massive bulk would be steered by a solid, cast steel 'plate' rudder 78ft 8in tall and weighing just over 101 tons.

On the day of the launch, 31 May 1911, the VIPs present included Lord Pirrie, J. Pierpont Morgan and J. Bruce Ismay, but it was not such a grand affair as one might suppose. The *Titanic* followed White Star policy of not being formally named or sent on its way with champagne; merely the trigger was simply released at the appointed time of 12.15pm and her slipway mass of 24,000 tons, with a pressure on the launching ways of 3 tons/sq in, took just 62 seconds to glide into the waters of the River

ABOVE *Titanic* almost ready for launching, her name chalked-in to show its position for later painting. Planking is piled in the foreground, ready to build the launching platform. *(UFTM H1560)*

ABOVE In case there was a hitch in *Titanic*'s launching, a battery of hydraulic rams were installed under her bow to give the sliding ways a shove.
(UFTM H1566)

RIGHT Launched to 'great jubilation' in one minute just after midday on 31 March 1911.
(UFTM H1558)

ABOVE At rest after her launch, the great liner still has part of the launch cradle (the fore poppet) attached to her bow. At this stage she is still almost identical to her sister ship, before later changes were made.
(UFTM H1569A)

LEFT In an advanced stage of fitting-out, the liner's fourth funnel (the dummy) is yet to be erected.
(UFTM MS503)

Lagan to the accompaniment of some 100,000 cheering onlookers. It had taken the application of more than 22 tons of tallow, engine oil and soft soap spread over the launching ways to enable the ship's huge hull to slide down the gradual slope to the water. As she became afloat for the first time, 160 tons of drag chains arrested the *Titanic*'s sternward momentum and brought her to a gradual halt. Tugs then took her alongside her fitting-out berth.

It was here that her two sets of four-cylinder, inverted direct-acting, triple expansion steam reciprocating engines were installed on the

BELOW *Titanic*'s master. A casual study of Captain (Commander, RNR) E.J. Smith relaxing with a cigar and a passenger's Borzoi hound. *(Topfoto)*

bedplates. In addition to these engines there was also a massive Parsons turbine, 24 double-ended and 5 single-ended Scotch boilers, piping, plumbing wiring and auxiliaries. The boilers were arranged in 6 entirely independent and isolated boiler rooms and the uptakes from these 6 boiler rooms ran into 3 funnels, the aftermost fourth being a dummy. Other fittings included fans, generators, steering gear, ovens, condensers, evaporators and the refrigeration plant. Interior furnishings included panelling, chairs, paintings, palms and lifts. For First Class passengers the *Titanic* boasted a squash rackets court, a Turkish bath, a fully equipped gymnasium, a swimming pool, a Parisian-style café and libraries staffed by librarians. Indeed, some suites on the *Titanic* had private promenade space at a cost of £870 during the high season. First Class passengers also enjoyed inclusive meals served in the Jacobean-style dining room; to dine in the à la carte Louis XIV restaurant, panelled in French walnut, was at the payment of a supplement.

The propellers were fitted in the Thompson Graving Dock and the entire fitting-out period lasted some ten months in all. With a gross tonnage of 46,328, an overall length of 882ft 9in and a beam of 92ft 6in, the *Titanic* was the largest moving object that had ever been constructed by man.

Entry into service

After trials, in which she achieved some 21 knots (kt), the *Titanic* was handed over to the White Star Line on 2 April 1912, under the command of Captain Bartlett. When she reached Southampton she was taken over by Captain Edward J. Smith. White Star's senior and most experienced master, Captain Smith was due to retire but had been persuaded to stay on and command the *Titanic* on her maiden voyage. He was the highest paid man at sea at the time, earning £1,250 a year plus a bonus of £1,000, if he returned his ships in good order.

The *Titanic* sailed from Belfast on 3 April with a skeleton crew of 120. Coincidental with her entry into service, and a potential threat to the *Titanic*'s sailing schedule, was the latter stages of a protracted coal-miners' strike. With coal in very short supply, the *Titanic* had about 1,880 tons of her total capacity of 8,000 tons when she arrived at Southampton. During the 570-mile trip from Belfast to Southampton she underwent further trials and machinery adjustment, and at one stage achieved the high speed of 23¼kt.

The lack of coal was further aggravated by a smouldering fire in No. 10 bunker on the starboard side of Boiler Room No. 6, which ignited when the ship left Belfast. Often coal sluices, through which the coal passed to the bunkers, caused combustion, a

conflagration easily extinguished by hoses. Notwithstanding this, Southampton's Board of Trade nautical surveyor, Maurice Harvey Clarke, granted the *Titanic* a Certificate of Seaworthiness. It was the largest ship he had to survey during his career to that date and he carried out three inspections. Even so, the unchecked fire smouldered on unabated for a further ten days throughout her maiden voyage until 12 April.

While at Southampton for the week, the *Titanic* burned some 415 tons of coal to run the steam-driven generators and the

Joseph Bruce Ismay

Chairman of the White Star Line

Joseph Bruce Ismay was born in 1862, the son of Thomas Henry Ismay, founder and chairman of the Oceanic Steam Navigation Company, popularly known as the White Star Line. On his father's death in 1899, J. Bruce Ismay took over as chairman and managing director of the company and instigated the building of four ships of the Adriatic Class, each in turn becoming the largest in the world.

In 1902 he oversaw the White Star Line's sale to the American International Mercantile Marine Company, although the British line retained a certain autonomy, flew the British flag and was still run by Ismay, who also became president of IMMCo.

In 1907 Ismay and Lord Pirrie of Harland & Wolff conceived the Olympic Class: two large ships (later extended to three) that would eclipse all competition in size and luxury, but not in speed.

Ismay had been enthusiastic about the *Olympic* during her maiden voyage and had booked himself into one of *Titanic*'s suites for her first crossing. After the new liner struck an iceberg on the night of 14 April 1912, he helped many of the passengers into the lifeboats until, seeing an opportunity, climbed into Collapsible Boat 'C' himself, an act for which he was later pilloried. Ismay was unable to watch as his brand new ship slid beneath the waters of the North Atlantic.

In June 1913, Ismay resigned both as chairman of the White Star Line and president of IMMCo and, in later retirement, spent his time between his London and Irish homes. He died in London in 1937.

RIGHT Portrait of J. Bruce Ismay, chairman of White Star and president of IMMCo. *(Topham Picturepoint/Press Association Images)*

domestic hot water and heating facilities. All that week, in order that the *Titanic* should sail on her scheduled maiden voyage, coal was commandeered from other IMMCo ships, which included the *New York* and *Philadelphia*. More coal was obtained from other Southampton-inbound White Star liners such as the *Oceanic* and *Majestic*, which had bunkered extra supplies in the United States. In all, some 4,427 tons was gathered from these vessels.

In addition to Captain Smith, the *Titanic*'s Chief Officer was Henry Wilde, transferred from the *Olympic*. This last-minute appointment displaced William McMaster Murdoch to First Officer and Charles Herbert Lightoller to the position of Second Officer. The incumbent Second Officer, David Blair, reluctantly left the ship. The *Titanic* was installed with the latest Marconi Marine Wireless Telegraphy equipment and the Marconi Marine Radio Officers were Jack Phillips and Harold Bride.

The rumour that the *Titanic* was 'unsinkable' spread from the ship's publicity. The description of the 15 watertight doors, which divided her hull into 16 watertight compartments, read: '. . . is held in the open position by a suitable friction clutch, which can be instantly released by means of a powerful electro-magnet controlled from the Captain's bridge, so that in the event of an accident, or at any time when it may be considered advisable, the Captain can, by simply moving an electric switch, instantly close the doors throughout and make the vessel practically unsinkable.'

Or perhaps Captain Smith's earlier confident remarks when he commanded the *Adriatic* on her maiden voyage five years previously, which were: 'I cannot imagine any condition which would cause a ship to founder. I cannot conceive of any vital disaster happening to this vessel. Modern shipbuilding has gone beyond that.' He was now in command of a liner built at the zenith of shipbuilding technology and twice the size of the *Adriatic*; he had no reason to doubt the structural integrity of the *Titanic*.

J. Bruce Ismay, the chairman and managing director of White Star, represented the company on her maiden voyage and

Thomas Andrews, Harland & Wolff's managing director, was sailing as the builder's guarantee representative along with seven other Harland & Wolff employees.

Maiden voyage

Some 914 passengers embarked on *Titanic* at Southampton, which included 180 First Class, 240 Second Class and 494 Third Class. Quite a few passengers had been switched from other liners which lay idle in the port due to the coal strike. Some had even been transferred from the French liner *France*, likewise affected. Other passengers joined at Cherbourg and Queenstown, making a total of 1,320 – 329 in First Class, 285 in Second Class and 706 in Third Class or Steerage. Fares ranged from special suites for a single fare of £500 (there were two of these, one of which was occupied by Bruce Ismay) to a Third Class berth for about £8. An average First Class one-way fare was about £30; a Second Class passage about £12. These costs have to be taken in context: a skilled craftsman working on *Titanic* earned about £2 a week while an unskilled labourer earned about £1. In contrast,

it was estimated that the millionaires on board *Titanic* represented a total capital of at least £120 million.

The number of crew signed on was 900, which made a total capacity of 2,220 people. The *Titanic* carried 16 lifeboats, the maximum required for a vessel over 10,000 gross tons under 1894 Board of Trade Regulations, at the time. In addition, she carried four collapsibles, stowed on top of the Bridge. They were able to take 1,178 people in total.

During the week's stay at Southampton, the *Titanic* had been busy coaling ship from its donors and loading supplies, as well as signing on crew who were largely seafarers from that port. Such was the nature of her preparing to sail (she had been a day late leaving Belfast because of high winds) that she was not open for inspection to members of the public.

At noon on sailing day, 10 April 1912, the *Titanic* eased away from 44 Berth in the White Star Dock and the same phenomenon which

BELOW Pulling away just after midday on 10 April 1912. Captain Steele, White Star's Marine Superintendent in Southampton, sits on a baulk of timber, warmly wrapped in his coat and homburg hat, carefully watching the proceedings. *(Authors' Collections)*

OPPOSITE TOP This expertly retouched photo of *Olympic* (prepared as a demo for James Cameron's 1997 film, *Titanic*) shows what *Titanic* would have looked like leaving the White Star Dock. *(Authors' Collections)*

OPPOSITE BOTTOM After rounding 'The Knuckle' at the entrance to the White Star Dock, *Titanic* turns before heading down the River Test to Southampton Water. An observer watches from the *Oceanic* or *New York*. *(Authors' Collections)*

had drawn the *Hawke* to the *Olympic* a year before, began to manifest itself again. The shallow water effect or 'canal effect' caused by the movement of *Titanic*'s large displacement as she was under way, resulted in the nearby *New York*, moored outboard of the *Oceanic*, to be dragged away from her moorings towards the *Titanic* as she was passing the strikebound liner. As the *New York* strained at her moorings, the 3in steel cable snapped and whipped through

ABOVE At a standstill off Berth 38. The American Liner *New York* had been moored in tandem outboard the White Star liner *Oceanic,* but the water displaced by the passing *Titanic* pulled her away and a collision seemed almost inevitable. The *Titanic* stopped, the *New York* was towed to safety and the *Titanic* carried on her way – one hour late. *(Authors' Collections)*

BELOW Presenting a picture of perfect Edwardian elegance, *Titanic* steams down Southampton Water with one tug (out of picture) for company, and passes a Union Castle liner laid up off the Military Hospital at Netley. *(Authors' Collections)*

ABOVE After passing Cowes on the Isle of Wight the liner picks up speed as she heads eastwards towards the Nab Lightship, the English Channel and Cherbourg. *(Peter Pearce)*

BELOW Eighteen-year-old Madeleine Force met and married John Jacob Astor IV, the richest man in the United States, in 1911. She survived the sinking of the *Titanic*, which claimed the lives of her husband and his valet. Madeleine was only 19 years of age, and had been married to Astor for just seven months. *(AP/Press Association Images)*

the air, fortunately not hitting anybody. Prompt action on Captain Smith's part in reversing the port propeller and attendant tugs averted a collision.

The slight delay caused by this incident made the *Titanic* late at Cherbourg, where a number of wealthy American passengers, including John Jacob Astor, inconvenienced by the hold-up, embarked. The following day the *Titanic* anchored off Queenstown in southern Ireland, where two tenders brought the last passengers and mail aboard, before heading out into the Atlantic. The *Titanic*'s route followed the southern track (arc) across the Atlantic to avoid icebergs that were normally prevalent in the northern track. By the 12th, *Titanic*'s bunker fire had finally been extinguished.

The *Titanic* was Captain Smith's 14th White Star command and he was due to retire after this trip. He held a commission as a commander in the Royal Naval Reserve (RNR), and as other officers of the crew were also in the RNR, the *Titanic* was entitled to fly the Blue Ensign. In a lifetime at sea Captain Smith had met most situations and he was respected as a navigator and a seaman, and was also popular with regular White Star passengers.

OPPOSITE Many distinguished people, both British and American, sailed on the *Titanic*. Among them were several American millionaires, who represented collectively some £100 million of capital – the equivalent today of more than £5.7 billion. *1. Bruce Ismay, Chairman of the White Star Line (survived); 2. Major A. Peuchen, Canadian Rifles (survived); 3. Major A.W. Butt, aide-de-camp to President Taft (died); 4. C.M. Hays, President of the Grand Trunk Railway (died); 5. Mrs J.J. Astor (survived); 6. Colonel J.J. Astor, multi-millionaire (died); 7. Lady Cosmo Duff-Gordon, also known as 'Lucille', fashion designer, (survived); 8. Jack Phillips, wireless operator on the Titanic (died); 9. The Countess of Rothes (survived); 10. Daniel Warren Marvin, son of the founder of the Biograph Company (died); 11. Mrs Mary Marvin, wife of Daniel (survived); 12. W.T. Stead, distinguished journalist (died); 13. Benjamin Guggenheim, American multi-millionaire mine owner (died); 14. Karl H. Behr, lawn tennis player (survived); 15. Isidor Straus, American multi-millionaire owner of Macy's (died). (Illustrated London News)*

ON BOARD THE "TITANIC" IN THE GREAT DISASTER: NOTABLE PASSENGERS.

RIGHT A lady in First
Class glances with
delicate curiosity at
one of the passenger
tenders as it disgorges
its cargo of emigrants
into the giant liner
while at anchor off
Queenstown. An
emergency boat is
slung out over the
liner's port side in case
of an urgent need.
(The Cork Examiner)

With a smooth crossing for the time of year, Captain Smith had the *Titanic*'s speed brought up to 21½kt. Through experience it was 'custom and practice' to push a vessel at full speed if weather conditions permitted. Most Atlantic masters frequently did so in order to maintain the regular advertised sailing schedules. There was no need not to steam at full speed; after all, not many liners collided with icebergs and the chance of meeting a small one (a 'growler') in the vast Atlantic, was negligible. Passing other liners was more common.

The south track should have been safe, but the winter of 1912 had been particularly mild in the Arctic and the ice flow had drifted south on the Labrador current, further south than anyone could remember. Safe navigation and the avoidance of collision relied upon deduced (dead) reckoning, the ship's chronometer and extra vigilance from the lookouts; in fog 'pebble splash and dog bark' would be the other instincts on which to draw. On the night of 14 April the *Titanic* was south-east of

BELOW Second Class passengers stroll about their promenade section of the Boat Deck while *Titanic* is at Queenstown, disembarking some passengers and last-minute mail while loading Irish emigrants and mails. *(Topfoto)*

The crow's-nest lookouts, Frederick Fleet and Reginald Lee, were told to keep a sharp look out for ice.

At 10:55pm, the Leyland Line's cargo-passenger ship *Californian* had stopped due to a heavy ice field surrounding it. The *Californian* was in the vicinity of the *Titanic's* position as her wireless signal, informing all ships that she was at a standstill, was strongly received and interrupted the *Titanic's* routine radio transmissions. The *Titanic's* Radio Officer acknowledged the *Californian's* signal, replying: 'Keep out! Shut up! You're jamming my signal, I'm working Cape Race.' At 11:35pm, Cyril Evans, the *Californian's* Radio Officer, shut down his radio set for the night (this was standard operating procedure for the day).

The *Titanic* powered on at 21½kt – the sea conditions on that dark, starlit night being cold and calm – with no reduction in speed as was custom and practice, towards the ice field that surrounded her.

By 11:30pm, most of the *Titanic's* passengers had turned in for the night but there would always be a few revellers and card players who remained.

About a minute before 11:40pm, Fleet spotted a dark object looming some 500yd in the distance in the *Titanic's* path. He rang the bell three times and phoned the Bridge to report: 'Iceberg right ahead.' The ship had about 30 seconds in which to turn. First Officer William Murdoch moved the Bridge telegraph to 'Stop', then 'Full Astern', ordering 'Hard a starboard!' to evade the iceberg. This was the tiller order such that the helm and heading should be brought round to port. Although the *Titanic* veered around some 20° to port, it took some 30 seconds to answer her helm over a half of a mile. Murdoch also pressed the button to shut all watertight doors.

The *Titanic's* momentum carried her underway through the water and impacted with the iceberg on the starboard side of her hull. Beneath the water, from near the bow to 300ft further aft, a protruding 'spur' of ice from the berg 'pecked' at the hull, exerting a very high concentrated pressure as it made contact. Thus, a series of glancing impacts caused the rivets to fail and fracture ('pop') under the sudden increased loading. Consequently the

Newfoundland, pushing at full speed through the cold waters of the Atlantic.

Around 12:00 (noon) on 14 April, while steaming westerly at a little over 21½kt, Captain Smith altered course further south based on ice reports being radioed in. Later in the evening of that day a further nine ice-warning messages were received from other vessels. The *Titanic* received a signal from the steamer *Mesaba*, which radioed a position in the *Titanic's* track, that she had encountered heavy field ice and several large icebergs. Apparently the message was neither delivered to the navigational personnel nor posted on the Bridge, as was the protocol. Another steamer, the *Rappahannock*, signalled at 10:30pm that she had passed several large icebergs and heavy field ice and had also sustained damage to her rudder. The Radio Officer acknowledged this signal.

seams tore and, in addition, the plate caulking broke below the waterline. All this happened intermittently as the hull scraped past the spur. The area laid open to the sea was later estimated by H&W's Edward Wilding, at the enquiry, to be 12sq ft. Through the gap in the plates the sea water entered and flooded the watertight compartments.

Subsequent forensic analysis on wreckage recovered from the site pinpointed the wrought-iron rivets, which had been formed with slag in them and were susceptible to 'brittle fracture'. In other words, at sustained lower temperatures they had a low resistance to sudden impact or, from being fairly tough at normal sea temperatures, had become brittle at freezing temperatures. Also, the nature of rivets is that they are designed to resist failure in a shear mode. During impact with the iceberg the rivets would have been submitted to a sudden

load in tension (a tensile mode). The *Titanic* had been steaming through sea-water temperatures as low as -2ºC (28º–30ºF) for some time before the impact.

The *Titanic*'s hull, like that of the *Olympic*, was divided by 15 transverse bulkheads, extending well above the waterline, into 16 watertight compartments. She had been designed to float with any two or the first four compartments from the bow flooded. In addition, she had a cellular double bottom, but the collision and subsequent gashes occurred above this. The damage sustained by the iceberg caused the first five watertight compartments to be exposed to flooding. The compartments extended from the cellular double bottom of the ship to five decks above, fore and aft. But from the third bulkhead to the ninth, extended up to the fourth deck above. As each compartment, working aft from the bow, filled, the bow sunk deeper, and

ABOVE Billed as the last picture ever taken of the *Titanic* as she leaves Queenstown, photographed by Father Francis Browne. He had an invitation to stay on the liner but his superior telegraphed 'Get off that ship!' *(Father Browne Collection: Society of Jesus, Dublin)*

The Russian East Asiatic S.S. Co.   Radio-Telegram.

S.S. "Birma".

No Words.	Origin.Station.	Time handed in.	Via.	Remarks.
beg 10 6.	Titanic	11 H.45M.April 14/15 1912.		Distress call Liga Loud.

Sgd - Sos. from M. G. Y.

We have struck iceberg sinking fast come to our assistance.

Position Lat. 41.46 n. Lon. 50.14. W.

M.G.Y.

sea water flowed over the top of the bulkheads.
With five compartments flooded the ship
could not survive. Indeed, Thomas Andrews's
snap judgement, along with the ship's
carpenter John Hutchinson, of the situation,
estimated that the liner had just over an hour to
live before foundering.

Captain Smith ordered the Radio Officers
to send out the regular international distress
call for help, CQD at 12:10am on 15 April,
while passengers were aroused to muster at
the lifeboats.

Although the *Titanic*'s position was
thought to be some 19½ miles from the silent
Californian, it was Captain Arthur Rostron of
Cunard's *Carpathia* whose radio picked up the
distress call. He turned the *Carpathia* about
and ordered 'Full Steam Ahead', a maximum of
17kt, to the *Titanic*'s last reported position. He
radioed back that he estimated he would be
there in four hours' time. So the little *Carpathia*

LEFT 25-year old John 'Jack' Phillips was the Senior Wireless Operator on the *Titanic*. Being employed by the Marconi Company his main duties included sending and receiving passengers' telegrams. Ship-related messages were also dealt with and one message from the *Mesaba,* which told of where ice was expected, did not get through to the Bridge because of the volume of passenger wireless traffic. *(Topfoto)*

ABOVE The last breakfast menu served in Third Class. *(AP Photo/Chitose Suzuki)*

RIGHT Shortly after the sinking icebergs were photographed near the scene of the disaster. *(US Library of Congress)*

LEFT The Cunard liner *Carpathia* was on her way to the Mediterranean when she picked up *Titanic*'s distress calls. She turned about and gallantly raced through the night, arriving in time only to pick up survivors. *(Authors' Collections)*

ABOVE Engelhardt collapsible boat 'D' approaches the rescue ship, *Carpathia*, of the Cunard Line. *(Topfoto)*

OPPOSITE The *New York Times* was the first to break the actual news of the disaster, other papers only having guessed what had happened. This front page was eventually cast in bronze and displayed outside the *NYT* offices in New York. *(The Granger Collection/Topfoto)*

BELOW As news arrived of the tragedy anxious crowds gathered outside White Star offices such as the one seen here in London. *(The Granger Collection/Topfoto)*

went crashing through the same dark night and calm sea, icebergs or no icebergs, on a mission of mercy.

When the first lifeboat was lowered it contained 27 passengers and crew, less than half its capacity of 65 (perhaps 10 more at a squeeze in a calm sea). Between 12:45am and 2:05am, the officers and crew managed to lower 18 of the *Titanic*'s 20 lifeboats.

By 2:10am the stern of the *Titanic* had risen out of the sea to an angle of 80°, but the generators were still running to light the ship. Below decks order became chaos; anything not fixed or fastened in place moved towards the bow. From later reports, high stresses experienced by the main deck caused the hull to split in two, just forward of the fourth funnel through the after expansion joints. The forward section quickly sank, as the stern settled back for a few seconds, before it again rose to the vertical position; at first remaining motionless before it began its plunge to the Atlantic floor 2½ miles below.

Of the 1,320 passengers and 900 crew, 706 survivors were rescued by the *Carpathia*. Only 339 bodies were recovered from the sea. The sinking had claimed the lives of Captain Smith and Thomas Andrews. J. Bruce Ismay was more fortunate; he managed to get into Engelhardt Collapsible 'C', but did not look back at the sinking liner he owned. For surviving he was vilified in the press, especially in the United States, foremost among his detractors being those newspapers owned by Randolph Hearst. As a mark of respect to Thomas Andrews and the seven guarantee team of workmen who had lost their lives in the disaster, Harland & Wolff closed the shipyard for the day on Saturday 20 April 1912.

At the subsequent Board of Trade enquiry into the loss of the *Titanic*, Edward Wilding, Andrews's deputy, was called to represent the builders, Harland & Wolff. Wilding presented his evidence in a clear and concise manner after being lambasted by hours of questions regarding the technical and theoretical detail of the ship. They mainly concerned what had happened during the sinking, and the *Titanic*'s perceivable survivability following its collision with the iceberg. Wilding's stability and trim calculations were based on empirical formula

"All the News That's Fit to Print."

The New York Times.

THE WEATHER.

Unsettled Tuesday; Wednesday, fair, cooler; moderate southerly winds, becoming variable.

For full weather report see Page 23.

VOL. LXI...NO. 19,595.   NEW YORK, TUESDAY, APRIL 16, 1912.—TWENTY-FOUR PAGES.   ONE CENT In Greater New York, Jersey City, and Newark. Elsewhere TWO CENTS.

TITANIC SINKS FOUR HOURS AFTER HITTING ICEBERG; 866 RESCUED BY CARPATHIA, PROBABLY 1250 PERISH; ISMAY SAFE, MRS. ASTOR MAYBE, NOTED NAMES MISSING

Col. Astor and Bride, Isidor Straus and Wife, and Maj. Butt Aboard.

"RULE OF SEA" FOLLOWED

Women and Children Put Over in Lifeboats and Are Supposed to be Safe on Carpathia.

PICKED UP AFTER 8 HOURS

Vincent Astor Calls at White Star Office for News of His Father and Leaves Weeping.

FRANKLIN HOPEFUL ALL DAY

Manager of the Line Insisted Titanic Was Unsinkable Even After She Had Gone Down.

HEAD OF THE LINE ABOARD

J. Bruce Ismay Making First Trip on Gigantic Ship That Was to Surpass All Others.

The admission that the Titanic, the biggest steamship in the world, had been sunk by an iceberg and had gone to the bottom of the Atlantic, probably carrying more than 1,400 of her passengers and crew with her, was made at the White Star Line offices, 9 Broadway, at 8:30 o'clock last night. Then P. A. S. Franklin, Vice President and General Manager of the International Mercantile Marine, conceded that probably only those passengers who were picked up by the Cunarder Carpathia had been saved. Advices received early this morning tended to increase the number of survivors by 200.

The admission followed a day in which the White Star Line officials had been optimistic in the extreme. At no time was the admission made that every one aboard the huge steamer was not safe. The ship itself, it was confidently asserted, was unsinkable, and inquirers were informed that she would reach port, under her own steam probably, but surely with the help of the Allan liner Virginian, which was reported to be towing her.

As the day passed, however, with no new authentic news from the Titanic or any of the ships which were known to have responded to her wireless call for help, it became apparent that no authentic news of the disaster probably could come only from the Titanic's steamer ship, the Olympic. The wireless range of the Olympic is 800 miles. That of the Carpathia, the Parisian, and the Virginian is much less, and as they neared the position of the Titanic they drew further and further out of short range. From the Titanic's position at the time of the disaster it is doubtful if any of the ships except the Olympic could establish communication with shore.

Titanic Sank at 2:20 A. M. Monday.

In the White Star offices the hope was held out all day that the Parisian and the Virginian had taken off some of the Titanic's passengers, and efforts were made to get into communication with these liners. Until such communication was established the White Star officials refused to recognize the Titanic's passengers aboard them.

But by nightfall came the message from Capt. Haddock of the Olympic to Cape Race, Newfoundland, telling of the foundering of the Titanic and of the rescue of 655 of her passengers by the Cunarder Carpathia, which, the wireless message said, reached the position of the Titanic at daybreak. All they found there, however, was lifeboats and wreckage. The biggest ship in the world had sunk at 2:20 o'clock yesterday morning.

Mr. Franklin admitted late last night that the Parisian and the Virginian, though they were among the first to answer the Titanic's calls for help, could not have reached the scene before 10 o'clock yesterday morning, seven and a half hours after the big Titanic buried her nose beneath the waves and pitched downward out of sight. The Carpathia, so the wireless dispatch from Capt. Haddock to Cape Race announced, reached the scene of the Titanic's foundering at daybreak, several

The Lost Titanic Being Towed Out of Belfast Harbor.

CAPT. E. J. SMITH, Commander of the Titanic.

hours before the expected arrival of the Virginian and the Parisian.

THE PROBABLE LOSS.

1,405 Lives Lost First Report.

It is unbelievable, so White Star Line officials were compelled to concede finally, that the Carpathia should have failed to pick up every lifeboat which still floated on the waves. If they failed to pick up more than 655 passengers, it was because the others of the ship's complement had gone with her to the bottom.

But it was not until nearly nightfall that the extent of the disaster was realized. Before that the reassuring nature of the bulletins issued by the White Star line was sufficient to quiet the fears of those who had relatives or friends aboard the unfortunate ship and to prevent, so general belief in a serious disaster.

Capt. Haddock of the Olympic, which is printed in another column of THE TIMES, strongly indicated that none but the 655 taken from life boats by the Carpathia had been saved. This message was re-

THE PROBABLE LOSS.
Number Aboard.

First cabin	325
Second cabin	285
Steerage	710
Crew (estimated)	900
Total	2,200
Saved.	
By the Carpathia	866
Probably drowned	1,384

layed immediately to the White Star offices, but Mr. Franklin positively declined to make the text of the message public. He offered still the hope that passengers were aboard the Parisian and the Virginian, and even when the admission was wrung from him that there seemed little hope of the saving of any others than the 655 aboard the Carpathia, he clung to the hope that in some unexplained way there were other passengers aboard the two Allan liners.

First Reported Titanic in Tow.

Throughout the day there had been reassurances that the Titanic was being towed to port by the Virginian,

POLAND WATER promotes Health. Avoid contagion by drinking purest water in world. Off. 1,183 B'way. Tel. Mad. Sq. 6786—Adv.

PARTIAL LIST OF THE SAVED.

Includes Bruce Ismay, Mrs. Widener, Mrs. H. B. Harris, and an Incomplete name, suggesting Mrs. Astor's.

Special to The New York Times.

CAPE RACE, N. F., Tuesday, April 16.—Following is a partial list of survivors among the first-class passengers of the Titanic, received by the Marconi wireless station this morning from the Carpathia, via the steamship Olympic:

Mrs. JACOB P. — and maid.
Mr. HARRY ANDERSON.
Mrs. ED. W. APPLETON.
Mrs. ROSE ABBOTT.
Miss G. M. BURNS.
Miss D. D. CASSEBERE.
Miss WM. M. CLARKE.
Mrs. B. CHIBNACK.
Miss E. G. CROSSBIE.
Miss H. ROSEBIE.
Miss JEAN HIPACK.
Mrs. H.T. B. HARRIS.
Mrs. ALEX. HALVERSON.
Miss MARGARET BAYS.
Mr. BRUCE ISMAY.
Mr. and Mrs. ED. KIMBERLEY.
Mr. F. A. KENNYMAN.
Miss EMILE KENCHEN.
Miss O. F. LONGLEY.
Mrs. A. F. LEADER.
Mrs. ERNEST LIVER.
Miss MARY CLINES.
Miss SINGRID LINDSTROM.
Mr. GUSTAVE J. LESNEUR.
Miss GIORGETTA A. MADILL.
Mme. MELICARD.
Mrs. TUCKER and maid.
Mrs. J. B. THAYER.
Mr. J. B. THAYER, Jr.
Mr. HENRY WOOLMER.
Miss ANNA WARD.
Mr. RICHARD M. WILLIAMS.
Mrs. F. M. WARNER.
Mrs. HELEN A. WILSON.
Miss WILLARD.
Miss MARY WICKS.
Mrs. GEO. D. WIDENER and maid.
Mrs. J. STEWART WHITE.
Miss MARIE YOUNG.
Mr. THOMAS POTTER, Jr.
Mrs. EDNA S. ROBERTS.
Countess of ROTHER.

Mr. C. ROLMANE.
Mrs. SUSAN P. ROGERSON. (Probably Ryerson).
Miss EMILY B. ROGERSON.
Mrs. ARTHUR ROGERSON.
Master ALLISON and nurse.
Miss K. T. ANDREWS.
Miss NINETTE PANHART.
Miss E. W. ALLEN.
Mr. and Mrs. D. BISHOP.
Mr. H. BLANK.
Miss A. BASSINA.
Mrs. JAMES BAXTER.
Mr. GEORGE A. BATT
Miss G. BONNELL.
Mrs. J. M. BROWN.
Miss G. C. BOWEN.
Mr. and Mrs. E. L. BECK
Miss RUTH TAUSSIG.
Miss ELLA THOR.
Mr. and Mrs. E. Z. TAYLOR.
GILBERT M. TUCKER.
Mr. J. B. THAYER.
Mr. JOHN B. ROGERSON.
Mr. M. ROTHSCHILD.
Miss MADELEINE NEWELL.
Mrs. MARJORIE NEWELL.
HELEN W. NEWSON.
Mr. PIENNAD GOMOD.
Mr. E. C. OSTBY.
Miss HELEN R. OSTBY.
Mrs. MAMAN J. RENAGO.
Milk. OLIVIA.
Mrs. D. W. MERVIN.
Mr. PHILIP EMOCK.
Md. JAMES GOOGHT.
Miss RUBERTA MAIMY.
Mrs. MAMAN J. MARECHAL.
Mr. W. E. MINEHAN.
Miss APPIE RANELT.
Major ARTUR PEUCHEN.
Mr. KARL H. BEHR.
Miss DERSETTE.

Mrs. WILLIAM BUCKNELL.
Mrs. O. H. BARKWORTH.
Mrs. H. B. STEFFASON.
Mrs. ELSIE BOWERMAN.

The Marconi station reports that it missed the word after "Mrs. Jacob P." In a list received by the Associated Press this morning this name appeared well down, but in The Times list it is first, suggesting that the name of Mrs. John Jacob Astor is intended. This supposition is strengthened by the fact that, except for Mrs. H. J. Allison, Mrs. Astor is the only lady in the "A" column of the ship's passenger list attended by a maid.

NAMES PICKED UP AT BOSTON.

BOSTON, April 15.—Among the names of survivors of the Titanic picked up by wireless from the steamer Carpathia here to-night were the following:

Mr. and Mrs. J. HENRY.
Mr. W. A. HOOPER.
Mr. MILE.
Mr. J. FLYNN.
Miss ALICE FORTUNE.
Mrs. ROBERT DOUGLAS.
Miss HILDA SLAYTER.
Mr. P. SMITH.
Mrs. BRAHAM.
Miss LUCILLE CARTER.
Mr. WILLIAM CARTER.
Miss CUMMINGS.
Mrs. FLORENCE MARE.
Mrs. ALICE PHILLIPS.
Mrs. PAULA MUNGE.
Miss JANE —.
Miss PHYLLIS O. —.
HOWARD B. CASE.
Miss MINEHAN.
Miss BERTHA.

Is proceeding to New York direct. We very much fear that there has been serious loss of life, but it is impossible for us to say definitely concerning this and part of the situation until we are able to reassure ourselves whether or not any of the Titanic's passengers are aboard the Allan liners.

We are hopeful that the rumors which have reached us by telegraph from Halifax that there are passengers aboard the Virginian and the Parisian will prove to be true, and that these vessels will turn up with some of the passengers. It is the loss of life that makes this thing so awful. We can replace the money loss, but not the lives of those who went down.

Another version of the message from the Olympic was current last night and included the sentence: "Loss likely 1,800 souls." This sentence was not in the message received by The Times from Cape Race nor in that sent to the White Star line offices.

and when Capt. Haddock's message proved this to be untrue only the admission was made at the White Star offices that the Titanic had sunk. Mr. Franklin said that Capt. Haddock's message was brief and "neglected to say that all the crew had been saved." But the inference was not that all the passengers had been saved. Rather it was that many of them had died, and presently Mr. Franklin admitted the fear that there had been a terrible loss of life on the Titanic.

This version of Capt. Haddock's wireless had been given at the White Star offices:

Capt. Haddock of the Olympic sends a wireless message to the White Star offices that the steamer Titanic sank at 2:20 A. M., after all the passengers and crew had been lowered to life boats and transferred to the Virginian. The steamship Carpathia, with

CRETA CREME HAND SOAP. Instantly removes stains. Large Can 10c. —Adv.

several hundred passengers of the Titanic, is now en route to New York. At 9 o'clock, however, he modified this statement, declaring:

As far as we know the situation, there have been rumors from Halifax that three steamers were at the scene of the Titanic's sinking, namely, the Virginian, the Parisian, and the Carpathia. We have heard from Capt. Haddock of the Olympic, who says that the Titanic sank at 2:20 o'clock this morning. Haddock also informs us that the Carpathia has 675 survivors on board. It is very difficult to say whether the Virginian and the Parisian have any survivors on board until we can get a report from those vessels.

Fears Serious Loss of Life.

We have asked for that report from Capt. Haddock, and we are expecting a reply at any time. The Carpathia

GREAT BEAR SPRING WATER. 50c. per case of 6 glass-stoppered bottles.—Adv.

Biggest Liner Plunges to the Bottom at 2:20 A. M.

RESCUERS THERE TOO LATE

Except to Pick Up the Few Hundreds Who Took to the Lifeboats.

WOMEN AND CHILDREN FIRST

Cunarder Carpathia Rushing to New York with the Survivors.

SEA SEARCH FOR OTHERS

The California Stands By on Chance of Picking Up Other Boats or Rafts.

OLYMPIC SENDS THE NEWS

Only Ship to Flash Wireless Messages to Shore After the Disaster.

LATER REPORT SAVES 866.

BOSTON, April 15.—A wireless message picked up late to-night, relayed from the Olympic, says that the Carpathia is on her way to New York with 866 passengers from the steamer Titanic aboard. They are mostly women and children, the message said, and it concluded: "Grave fears are felt for the safety of the balance of the passengers and crew."

Special to The New York Times.

CAPE RACE, N. F., April 15.—The White Star liner Olympic reports by wireless this evening that the Cunarder Carpathia reached, at daybreak this morning, the position from which wireless calls for help were sent out last night by the Titanic after her collision with an iceberg. The Carpathia found only the lifeboats and the wreckage of what had been the biggest steamship afloat.

The Titanic had foundered at about 2:20 A. M., in latitude 41:16 north and longitude 50:14 west. This is about 30 minutes of latitude, or about 34 miles, due south of the position at which she struck the iceberg. All her boats are accounted for and about 655 souls have been saved of the crew and passengers, most of the latter presumably women and children.

There were about 2,100 persons aboard the Titanic.

The Leyland liner California is remaining and searching the position of the disaster, while the Carpathia is returning to New York with the survivors.

It can be positively stated that up to 11 o'clock to-night nothing whatever had been received at or heard by the Marconi station here to the effect that the Parisian, Virginian or other ships had picked up any survivors, other than those picked up by the Carpathia.

First News of the Disaster.

The first news of the disaster to the Titanic was received by the Marconi wireless station here at 10:25 o'clock last night [as told in yesterday's New York Times.] The Titanic was first heard giving the distress signal "C. Q. D.," which was answered by a number of ships, including the Carpathia.

ABOVE The lifeless body of a victim of the sinking is pulled from the Atlantic some time after the disaster. *(Authors' Collections)*

RIGHT Junior Wireless Operator Harold Bride being helped ashore in New York from the *Carpathia*. His feet had been badly injured while hanging on to overturned collapsible boat 'B'. *(The Granger Collection/Topfoto)*

BELOW A group of survivors on board *Carpathia* en route for New York. *(The Granger Collection/Topfoto)*

and the sequence of the events that resulted in the loss of the *Titanic* could not have been foreseen at the time. The degree of damage sustained and the manner in which it occurred had therefore been unimaginable, and therefore could not have been anticipated or allowed for. Shortly after the enquiry was concluded, during which Harland & Wolff was exonerated of any blame for the loss of the vessel.

Following the loss of the *Titanic*, the Board of Trade Regulations were changed to improve the safety of life at sea such that sufficient life-saving apparatus should be available for all passengers and crew. This was interpreted to mean that all those aboard a ship could be accommodated in half the lifeboats carried in the event of a list. In addition was the setting up in 1913 of the International Ice Patrol Service, managed by the United States, to which the UK contributed 30% of the total outlay. Its function consisted of locating all ice threatening the steamship tracks, such as drifting icebergs in the sea lanes, and placing that information in the hands of every steamship master by means of wireless telegraphy. Together with a Gulf of St Lawrence Ice Patrol Service, regular bulletins on ice conditions and recommendations as to the route to be followed were broadcast. The transatlantic shipping lanes were routed further south during the winter and spring months. Every vessel was required to be installed with wireless telegraphy to be manned continuously over a 24-hour period by competent radio officers or Marconi's own officers.

During a major rebuild, the *Olympic*'s watertight bulkheads were extended up to the main strength deck, as was the cellular double bottom. Similar modifications were made to the *Britannic* while under construction on the stocks.

The *Titanic* had been five years in the making and was at the cutting edge of naval architecture and marine engineering technology of the day; she was the epitome of Edwardian grandeur afloat. That said, it took only 2 hours 20 minutes for her complete destruction and its attendant loss of life. Lloyds of London paid out £1 million insurance for the loss of the *Titanic*'s hull.

Countdown to disaster – 1912

10 April	12:15pm	*Titanic* departs White Star Dock, Southampton, on maiden voyage.
	6:35pm	Arrives at Cherbourg, France.
	8:10pm	Departs Cherbourg for Queenstown (Cobh), Ireland.
11 April	11:30am	Arrives Queenstown.
	1:30pm	Departs Queenstown.
12 April	Noon Friday (12th) to noon Saturday (13th) – 519 miles logged.	
13 April	Noon Saturday (13th) to noon Sunday (14th) – 546 miles logged.	
14 April	9:00am	*Caronia*, eastbound from New York to Liverpool, reports ice at 42° N, extending from Longitude 49° to 50°.
	1:42pm	*Titanic*'s position 42° 35'N, 49° 52'W.
	1:45pm	*Amerika* reports ice 41° 27'N, 50° 8'W.
	5:50pm	*Titanic* reaches 'The Corner', 42°N, 47°W. Changes course from S 62°W to S 86°W.
	7:00pm	Air temperature 43°F (8°C).
	7:15pm	Forward forecastle hatch secured to prevent glow interfering with the crow's-nest watch. Ice warning received from *Baltic* at 1.42pm posted on Bridge.
	7:30pm	Air temperature 39°F (4°C). *Californian* reports ice 42° 3'N, 49° 9'W.
	8:40pm	Officer of the Watch Charles Lightoller orders ship's carpenter Maxwell to watch the fresh-water supply as it may freeze.
	9:00pm	Air temperature 33°F (1°C)
	9:40pm	*Mesaba* warns of ice 42°N to 41° 25'N, 49°W to 50° 30'W, but warning not delivered to *Titanic*'s Bridge.
	10:00pm	First Officer William Murdoch relieves Second Officer Lightoller on the Bridge. Lookouts Lee and Fleet relieve Jewell and Symons in the crow's-nest. Air temperature reaches freezing – 32°F (0°C).
	10:30pm	Sea temperature reaches freezing. *Rappahannock* passes *Titanic* and reports by Morse lamp she has just run though heavy ice.
	11:00pm	*Californian* tries to warn of ice, but is cut off by *Titanic*'s wireless operator.
	11.40pm	*Titanic* collides with iceberg.
15 April	Midnight	Hogg and Evans relieve Lee and Fleet in crow's-nest.
	12:05am	Captain Smith orders lifeboats uncovered and crew mustered.
	12:10am	*Titanic*'s position estimated 41° 46'N, 50° 14'W.
	12:15am	*Titanic* broadcasts her first call for assistance – CQD.
	12:45am	First distress rocket fired. First lifeboat lowered. CQD wireless transmission upgraded to SOS.
	1:40am	Last rocket fired.
	2:05am	Last lifeboat lowered.
	2:10am	Last wireless signal transmitted.
	2:18am	*Titanic*'s lights fail.
	2:20am	*Titanic* founders; over 1,500 lives lost.

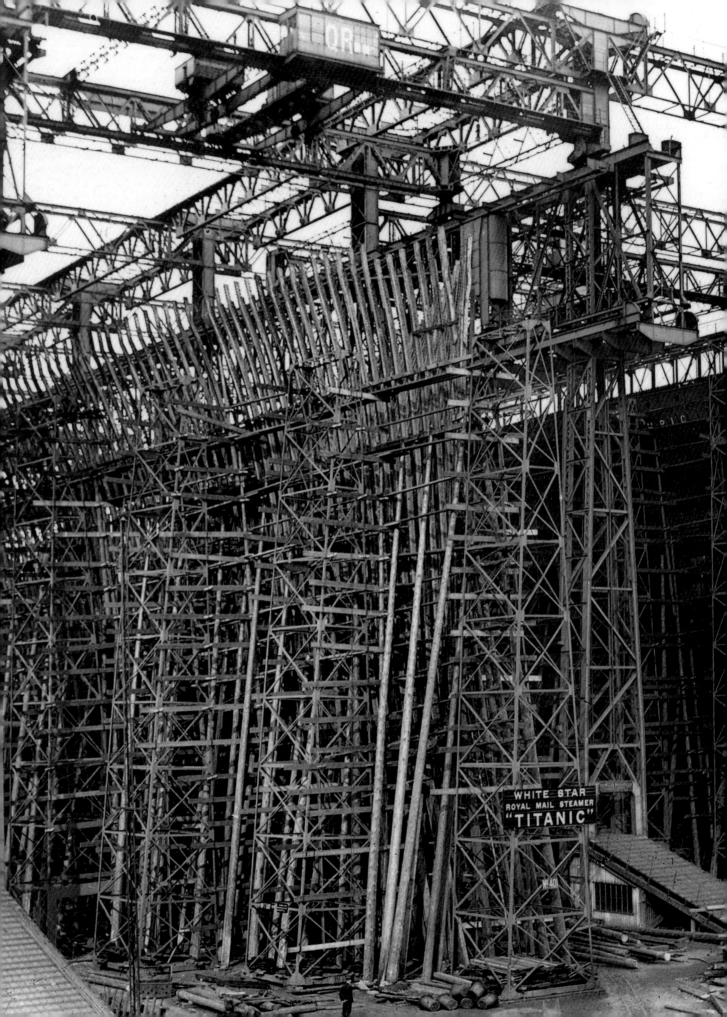

WHITE STAR
ROYAL MAIL STEAMER
"TITANIC"

Chapter Two

Anatomy of the *Titanic*

Titanic and her older sister, *Olympic*, exceeded in tonnage the previously largest ships in the world – Cunard's *Lusitania* and *Mauretania* – by 50 per cent and were over 100ft longer. The new White Star liners sacrificed speed in favour of size, luxury, space and comfort in an attempt to attract the cream of the first-class passenger trade on the North Atlantic.

The rising behemoths under Harland & Wolff's Arrol gantry, showing the starboard side of the *Titanic* (left), fully framed and slightly eclipsing the fully plated *Olympic* (right) on the adjacent slipway. *(UFTM H2377)*

ABOVE One of the two vaulted drawing offices at Harland & Wolff's works in Belfast, sited behind the main office block in Queen's Road and only a few yards from the Arrol gantry. It was here that skilled draughtsmen converted design concepts into detailed working drawings of the structure, machinery and electrical cabling layout of the new Olympic Class vessels. *(UFTM H1501)*

RIGHT The Arrol gantry was built over three original slipways. The *Olympic* can be seen to the left, built up to her tank tops, while *Titanic*'s building blocks can be clearly seen to the right. *(UFTM H1331)*

RIGHT Looking through the openings for watertight doors in the eight watertight bulkheads on the *Titanic*'s sister ship, *Britannic*. In the *Titanic* the watertight subdivision was designed so that if any two watertight compartments were flooded they would not compromise the safety of the ship. There were 15 transverse watertight bulkheads which extended from the double bottom to the upper deck at her forward end, and up as far as the saloon deck at her after end. Both extended far above the waterline. *(UFTM H1905)*

Hull

The *Titanic*'s construction was of the traditional keel, 300 frames, rib-and-beam type. Like the *Olympic*, she was constructed of mild steel with a cellular double bottom 5ft 3in deep. The area between the inner and outer layers was divided longitudinally by minor bulkheads with access manholes. The bottom plating was hydraulically riveted; the strakes were arranged in clincher fashion, with the edge of one plate overlapping the next. The underside of the framing was joggled so that the frame was indented to the thickness of the plating, thus ensuring that adjacent plates were level and avoiding the use of wedge-shaped inserts between the frame and plate.

In order to reduce the number of butts and overlaps to a minimum, plates of a large size for their day were chosen – some 2,000 in all. The shell plates were from 30ft to 36ft long and 6ft wide; the largest plates weighed some 4½ tons.

Steel plates used in the construction of the keel and the adjacent strakes were 1in thick, as were the plates at the waterline and the turn of bilge (where the bottom of the ship joined the ship's side). Plates used at the uppermost longitudinal strake of the hull were doubled for

RIGHT The massive stiffening of watertight bulkheads on the *Britannic* showing the vertical strengthening girders. The largest compartment on the *Titanic* was the Engine Room at 69ft long, and aft of this was the Turbine Room at 54ft long. Boiler rooms were mainly 57ft long with the exception of the one adjacent to the Engine Room which was 50ft long. *(UFTM H1906)*

Cutaway profile view of RMS *Titanic*.
(*Illustrated London News*)

Labels visible in image: WATER TIGHT BULKHEAD. Nº G · O.P. · O.P. · A · B · A · OUTER PLATING. · WEB FRAMES READY FOR INNER PLATING. · H1907. F.W.

extra strength. Some 3 million rivets were used in the overall construction.

The hull was subdivided by 15 transverse bulkheads, which created 16 watertight compartments. The watertight doors to these were electrically controlled from the Bridge and should any two of the largest compartments become flooded the vessel could remain afloat indefinitely. These safeguards led White Star to believe that the ship was practically unsinkable. However, on the night of her collision with an iceberg the starboard hull along the first five compartments was breached and laid open to the sea. Her watertight integrity was compromised and the ship's fate sealed.

Framing

The frames of a ship were as essential as the ribcage of a mammal for keeping its shape and form, and taking any exterior pressures without too much deformation of the main body while protecting all contained within.

On the Olympic Class, the 300 frames were spaced from 24in to 36in apart (the further forward or aft they were, the closer the spacing) and were formed from channel bar 10in deep with 3in flanges, and were about 66ft long. The frames at each end of the ship were of a built section of frame and reverse bar. The frames were pre-punched by machine with rivet holes (except in areas of excessive curvature of hull), heated in furnaces and bent to shape on bending slabs. This class of ship was framed using the 'transverse' system, giving the unplated frames the impression of ribs. Frame numbering, unusually, started amidships with a suffix of 'F' or 'A' to denote the forward or aft direction in which the frame was placed.

The frames were erected at the ship, with heels attached to the tank top that made up the ship's cellular double bottom – a pontoon made up of inner and outer bottoms with in-between 'floors' (vertical plating, pierced with manholes,

Following the post-*Titanic* structural modifications made to the *Olympic*, the *Britannic* embodied these new design features in her double bottom. Inner and outer skins were supported by lines of inner and outer frames. (UFTM H1912)

extending outwards and normal to the all-important keel) spaced at frame stations. The top of the frames terminated at the Strength Deck, in this case 'B' Deck – the Bridge Deck.

Plating

The plating that covered the frames was, in essence, the skin of the ship. Stiffened by the framing, it was strong and watertight and kept the elements out of the main structure.

The plates used in the construction of *Titanic* were rolled in as large a size as possible to reduce the number of riveted butt straps at the plate-to-plate joins and, in turn, reduce weight. Most of the plates were 6ft wide and 30ft long, their weights being between 2½ and 3 tons. The largest plates of 4¼ tons incorporated into the hull were 36ft long.

LEFT Hand riveters at work near the bow of the *Britannic*. The seeming lack of activity, apart from this group, indicates that this photograph may have been posed. Hand riveting was carried out where the hydraulic riveting machine could not reach. Some three million rivets were used in the construction of the *Titanic*'s hull, one-third of which were fastened with a hydraulic riveter. (UFTM H1915)

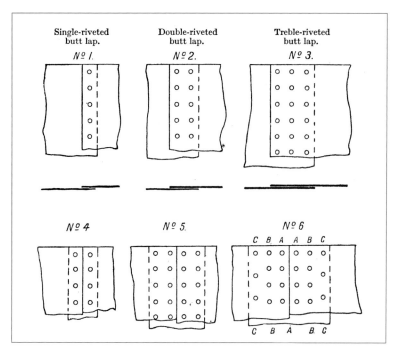

Single-riveted butt lap.	Double-riveted butt lap.	Treble-riveted butt lap.
No. 1.	No. 2.	No. 3.
No. 4.	No. 5.	No. 6.

ABOVE AND BELOW Different types of riveted joints employed on the *Titanic*'s hull plating. *(Authors' Collections)*

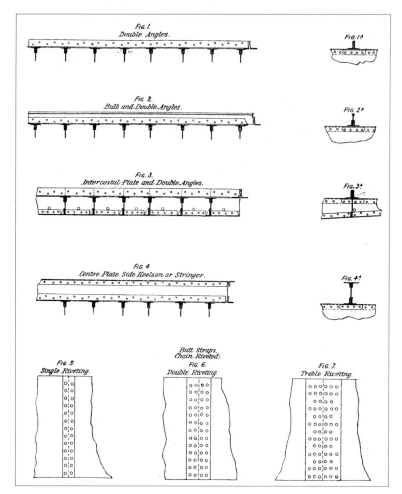

FIG. 1. Double Angles.
FIG. 1A

FIG. 2. Bulb and Double Angles.
FIG. 2A

FIG. 3. Intercostal Plate and Double Angles.
FIG. 3A

FIG. 4. Centre Plate Side Keelson or Stringer.
FIG. 4A

FIG. 5. Single Riveting.
FIG. 6. Butt Straps, Chain Riveted. Double Riveting.
FIG. 7. Treble Riveting.

ABOVE Riveting style No. 1. *(Authors' Collections)*

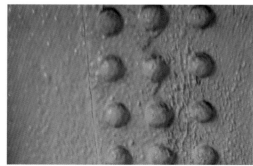

ABOVE Riveting style No. 3. *(Authors' Collections)*

Thicknesses of plating varied. The outer keel plate was 1½in (30/20in in shipbuilding terms) thick; the garboard strake (the strake next to the outer keel) was 1¼in (25/20in); and the rest of the plating up to the Strength Deck was 1in (20/20in) in thickness.

The shapes of the plates were taken from the half-block model and the scrieve board, but where difficult shapes were encountered moulds were made at the ship to get a true shape. Rivet holes were punched in the plate edges and through corresponding locations in the frames before the plate was lifted into position.

The bottom plating up to the turn of bilge was laid clinker fashion, and above the turn of bilge it was laid in the in-and-out format. Before riveting, the plates were fixed in place with bolts in every second or third rivet hole.

Water ballast

Water tanks filled the whole of the inside of *Titanic*'s double bottom. They were mainly used to carry water ballast to ensure the stability of the vessel at sea. A lightly loaded vessel floats higher in the water, making her less stable. To counteract this tendency the ballast

tanks are filled with water to weigh the ship down and increase her stability.

Under normal operating conditions when a vessel is loaded with cargo, stores and/ or passengers, the water ballast is gradually pumped out until her draught matches that when only the ballast is carried.

During the course of her voyage, the *Titanic's* boilers consumed coal while her passengers and crew enjoyed the stores and fresh water, making her lighter, causing her to rise in the water. To maintain her optimum draught and stability, water ballast would have been pumped into the tanks in her double bottom to keep her weight constant and to maintain stability.

Watertight bulkheads and doors

The watertight subdivision was designed in such a way that if any two watertight compartments were flooded they would not compromise the safety of the ship. Fifteen transverse watertight bulkheads extended from the double bottom to the Upper Deck at the forward end, and up as far as the Saloon Deck at the after end. Both decks reached far above the waterline.

The largest compartment was the Engine Room at 69ft long; aft of this was the Turbine Room at 54ft long. Boiler rooms were mainly 57ft long with the exception of the one adjacent to the Engine Room which was 50ft long. Watertight integrity was maintained by 11 watertight doors of the 'drop' type designed

LEFT Watertight doors on the *Olympic* in raised, open position during outfitting. The *Titanic's* watertight integrity was maintained by 11 watertight doors of the 'drop' type, designed by Harland & Wolff, which closed vertically downwards when activated. *(UFTM H1471)*

RIGHT The same watertight doors in lowered, closed position. In the Engine Room the doors were normally kept open to give access for the firemen and trimmers during the watch changeover, but in the event of an emergency all doors could be operated from the Bridge. *(UFTM H1487)*

by Harland & Wolff, which closed vertically downwards when activated.

Doors could be opened and shut manually by a simple cranking handle which operated a helical gear which turned the 'worm' on the end of a shaft that engaged with a 'worm wheel'. This then turned a horizontal shaft with a gear pinion in its middle that meshed with a vertical rack integral with the door.

The doors were normally kept open for the firemen and trimmers to have access during the watch changeover. In the event of an emergency all doors could be operated from the Bridge by the flick of a switch. Each door was held open by a friction clutch sensitively counterbalanced in such a way that a powerful electro-magnet whose solenoid was integral with a rod could pivot the rod and release it. When activated, the rod and counterbalance disengaged a pawl and ratchet mechanism that allowed the door to close slowly under its own weight. As a further precaution floats were installed beneath the floor plates, and in the event of water entering the compartments, these would automatically lift and close the doors if they had not already been shut.

An escape ladder was provided in each engine and boiler room and other compartments so that the closing of the watertight doors at any time did not seal crew members inside. Electric alarm bells near each door rang prior to the door closing.

Harland & Wolff's Olympic Class RMS *Titanic*
Technical specification

Owners	Oceanic Steam Navigation Company (White Star Line)
Official number	131428
Port of registry	Liverpool
Certificate	Foreign-going steamship passenger
Crew	900
Passengers	2,439
Length overall (loa)	882 ft 9in
Length between perpendiculars (lbp)	850ft 0in
Breadth extreme	92ft 6in
Depth moulded to Shelter Deck	64ft 3in
Depth moulded to Bridge Deck	73ft 3in
Keel to Navigating Bridge	104ft 0in
Funnels	4 (fourth funnel 'dummy')
Masts	2
Keel to top of funnels	175ft 0in
Load draught	34ft 6in
Gross tonnage (gt)	46,328
Displacement at load draught	52,250 tons
Block coefficient at load draught	0.685
IHP of reciprocating engines	30,000
Shaft HP of turbine engines	16,000
Boilers	29
Fuel	Coal
Consumption per day	825 tons
Outer propellers (wing shafts)	2 x 3-bladed 23ft 6in diameter
Inner (centre) propeller	1 x 4-bladed 16ft 6in diameter
Engines for outer shaft	2 x reciprocating 4-cylinder steam engines
Engine for inner shaft	Low-pressure Parsons turbine
Top speed	24kt at 75rpm
Anchors	2 bower at 8 tons 1 centre at 15½ tons
Cost	£2,000,000

Superstructure

On the Olympic Class there were two main superstructure decks, the Promenade Deck and Boat Deck, extending over a length of 550ft above the Strength Deck (Bridge Deck), with officers' quarters, gymnasium, boiler casing, raised roofs over public rooms, standing atop the Boat Deck much like the deckhouses of the sailing ship era. Although not part of the main superstructure, a Poop Deck (aft, 106ft long) and a forecastle (forward, 128ft long) were separated from the main superstructure by well decks. On *Titanic*, the First Class cabins and à la carte restaurant were extended out to the ship's sides on the Bridge Deck, giving larger rooms (some with private promenades) in these areas and making her that much more luxurious – as well as increasing her gross tonnage by 1,000 tons – than her sister.

The superstructure was built of material of lighter scantlings (measurements) than the main hull in order to save top weight. The decks and open spaces on Bridge, Promenade and Boat Decks, Forecastle and Poop Decks and atop the officers' quarters were planked for sound insulation and appearance.

Expansion joints

When a ship is in a seaway it experiences flexing of the hull known as hogging and sagging. Hogging occurs when the ship's ends are in wave troughs and the hull is supported amidships by a wave's crest. This condition has the effect of allowing the bow and stern to drop. When that wave passes and the ship is supported at bow and stern it is the amidships section which, relatively unsupported, tends to drop – this is sagging.

A ship's hull is built like a box girder – a steel box that, to alleviate stresses when in a seaway, is stiffened at each longitudinal corner. Additional stiffening was included in the *Titanic* by adding plates along her bilge to alleviate the problem of hogging and sagging. Anything built above this main hull girder – i.e. the superstructure – experienced flexing in a seaway and was susceptible to cracking. To alleviate this tendency to flex expansion joints were built into the superstructure. In

effect, these joints were 'splits' built into an upper deck and partially down the sides of the superstructure and they 'worked' by opening and shutting as the structure flexed. To maintain watertight integrity a complex system of leather strips and under-deck water-catching channels were constructed along and under the joint, the leather strips being secured by brass straps.

On the Olympic Class there were two such expansion joints, one placed just aft of the forward funnel, and the other placed aft of the third funnel. They were incorporated across the Boat and Promenade Decks, extending down to the level of the Strength Deck (Bridge Deck, Deck B).

The lower ends of the joints ended sharply. Because of serious cracking that occurred to the *Olympic* in January 1912 it was decided the third ship, *Britannic*, would have five joints with circular endings to distribute flexing-induced stresses.

Decks

Excluding the top of the officers' quarters there were 11 decks in total, full or partial, of which 8 were designed for passenger accommodation, public rooms, dining and promenading.

Boat Deck housed the lifeboats, as well as the Gymnasium, First and Second Class entrances, raised roofs over the First Class Lounge and Smoke Room, captain's and officers' quarters. At the forward end of the deck was the all-important Bridge and Wheelhouse. The open part of the deck was wood-covered.

Promenade Deck A was First Class only, containing cabins forward, an entrance, reading and writing rooms, lounge, Smoke Room, verandah and Palm Court. Wood covered the outside promenade decking.

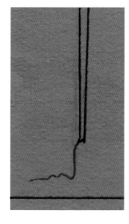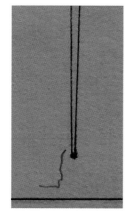

LEFT Drawings that show the cracks that occurred in the port aft and starboard aft expansion joints on the *Olympic*.
(Authors' Collections)

RIGHT A lone figure (often mistaken as Captain Smith, who would have been on the Bridge with the pilot at this stage) strolls along the Promenade Deck. An RMSP liner, preparing to head west, swings astern of the *Titanic*. *(Authors' Collections)*

Bridge Deck B was 550ft long, the upper deck of the hull girder. Cabins on this First Class deck (other than for the Second Class Smoke Room aft) had been extended outboard to the ship's side (as had the à la carte restaurant, its reception room, and the Café Parisian). Wood covered the promenades of the two private suites. Forward of the Bridge Deck, but separated by a well, were the raised forecastle (128ft), and the Poop Deck aft (106ft). From bow to stern was 882ft 9in in length.

Deck C, Shelter Deck, included the fore and aft well decks. Amidships, in between the well decks, was the majority of the First Class cabins; aft was the Second Class Library; crew were housed forward under the forecastle, and Third Class public rooms under the poop. Third Class promenaded in the after-well deck; hatches and electric cranes were in the fore well.

Deck D, Saloon Deck. The First Class Dining Saloon, Reception Room, and galley (the latter shared with Second Class) dominated the amidships third of this deck, with First Class cabins forward. Forward of a bulkhead was Third Class Open Space with firemen berthed forward of that. Aft were catering preparation spaces, the ship's hospital, Second Class dining, and then Second and Third Class accommodation.

Deck E, Upper Deck, contained accommodation for all classes, plus dormitories for trimmers, seamen, cooks and stewards. An engineers' mess was situated on the port side, aft of amidships.

Deck F, Middle Deck. This last complete deck accommodated Third Class forward and aft, and a Second Class section. Firemen were berthed right forward, stewards port amidships and engineers were berthed either side of the engine casing (i.e. the bulkheads surrounding the reciprocating engines). The Third Class Dining Saloon was amidships which was described as being better than First Class on some of the old ships.

Deck G, Lower Deck, was 850ft long. At either end of the boiler, engine and turbine room casings there was an orlop (partial) deck.

Orlop Deck, sited forward and aft of the boiler, engine and turbine rooms, had cargo, baggage and motor cars stowed forward, with refrigerated and other cargo placed aft.

Lower Orlop, placed forward beneath the Orlop Deck, provided cargo space.

The Tank Top, the top of the cellular platform, provided a platform on which sat the boilers, reciprocating engines, turbines and electrical generators. Forward was cargo and a firemen's access tunnel that led from spiral stairways to their quarters on Decks D to G.

LEFT *Titanic*'s structure as completed to 'C' Deck. Note the riveters at the distant right-hand side of the casing opening. *(UFTM H2423)*

BELOW The basic structure of what will become the First Class Dining Saloon of the *Britannic*, showing tubular deck-supporting bare steel pillars. These will eventually be disguised by ornate wood columns. *(UFTM H1929)*

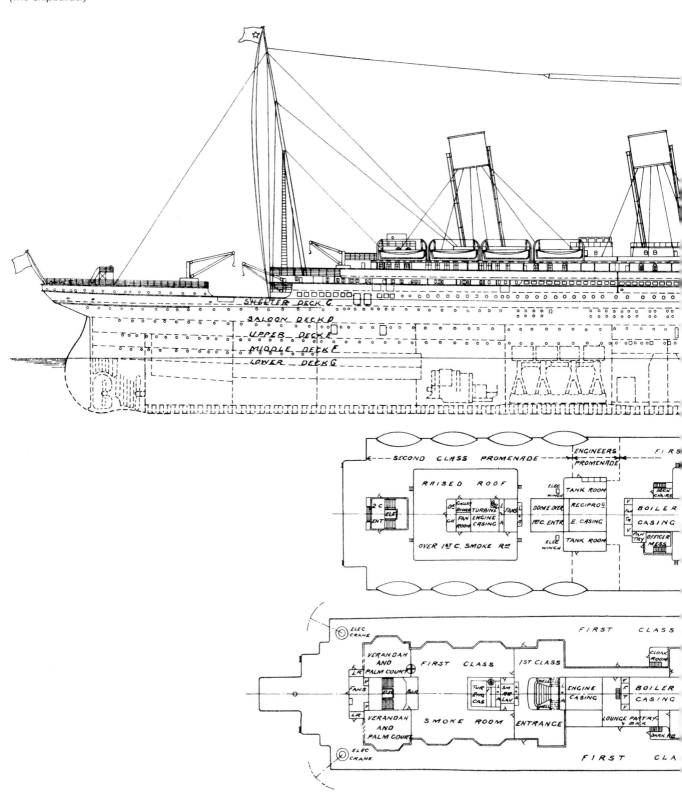

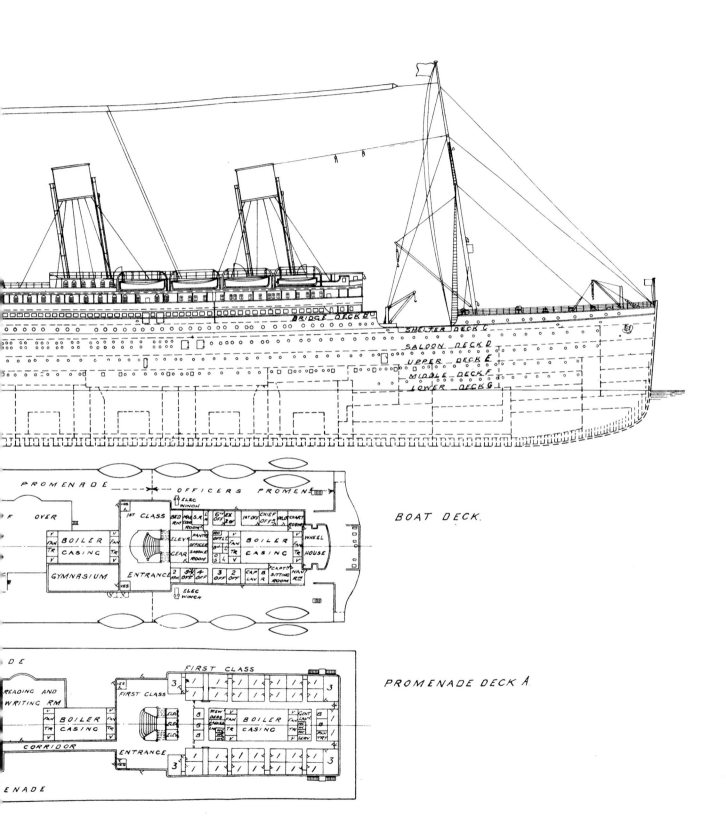

BRIDGE DECK B

SHELTER DECK C

SALOON DECK D

UPPER DECK E

MIDDLE DECK F

LOWER DECK G

PROMENADE — OFFICERS PROMEN.

BOAT DECK.

OVER

1ST CLASS

ELEC WINCH

BED RM

MAG S.R COM ROOM

6TH EX OFF 2 OF

1ST OFF

CHIEF OFF S

PILOT CHART ROOM

BOILER CASING

FAN TR

BOILER CASING

TR

ELEV GEAR

PANTO

OFFICER SMOKE ROOM

FAN V

WHEEL HOUSE

GYMNASIUM

ENTRANCE

2 OFF

3 & 4 OFF

3 OFF

CAP LAV

B LAV

CAPTN SITTING ROOM

NAV RM

ELEC WINCH

FIRST CLASS

PROMENADE DECK A.

DE

READING AND WRITING RM

FIRST CLASS

3

1

1

1

1

1

3

BOILER CASING

FAN TR

TR

STEW DESS CUPBD

FAN

BOILER CASING

FAN TR

GENT LAV

PRI PAN TRY SERV

CORRIDOR

ENTRANCE

3

1

1

1

1

1

3

ENADE

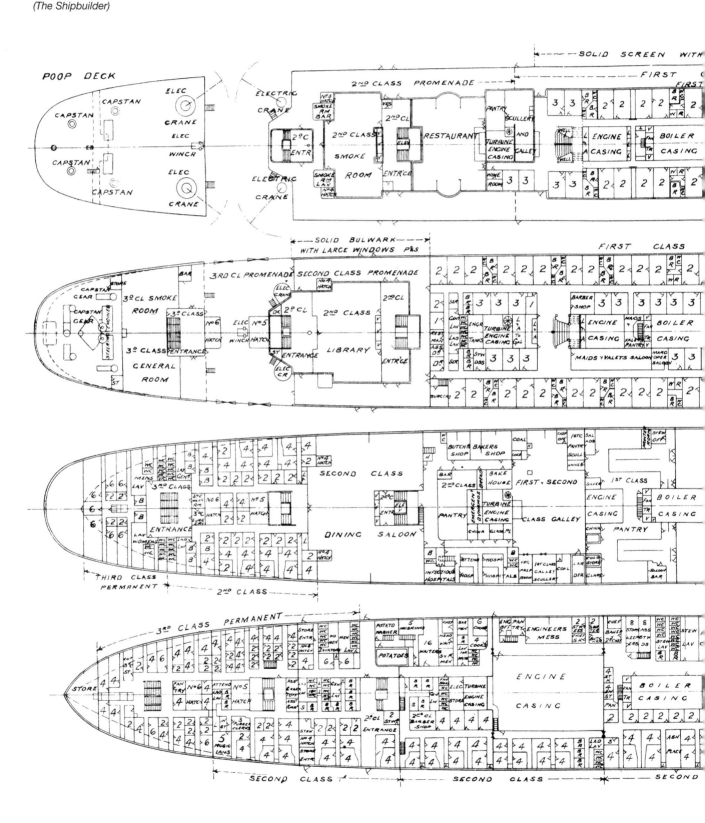

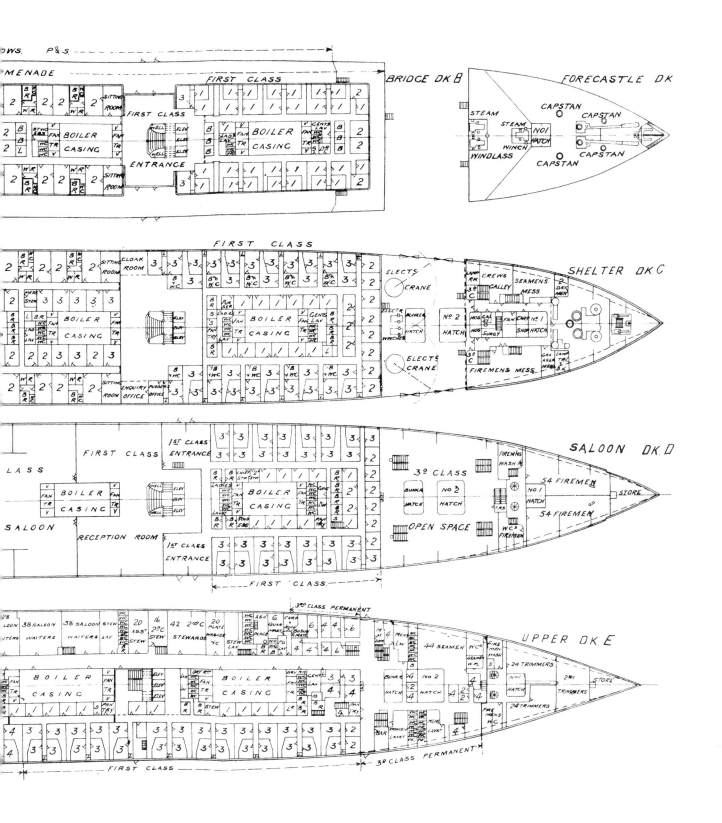

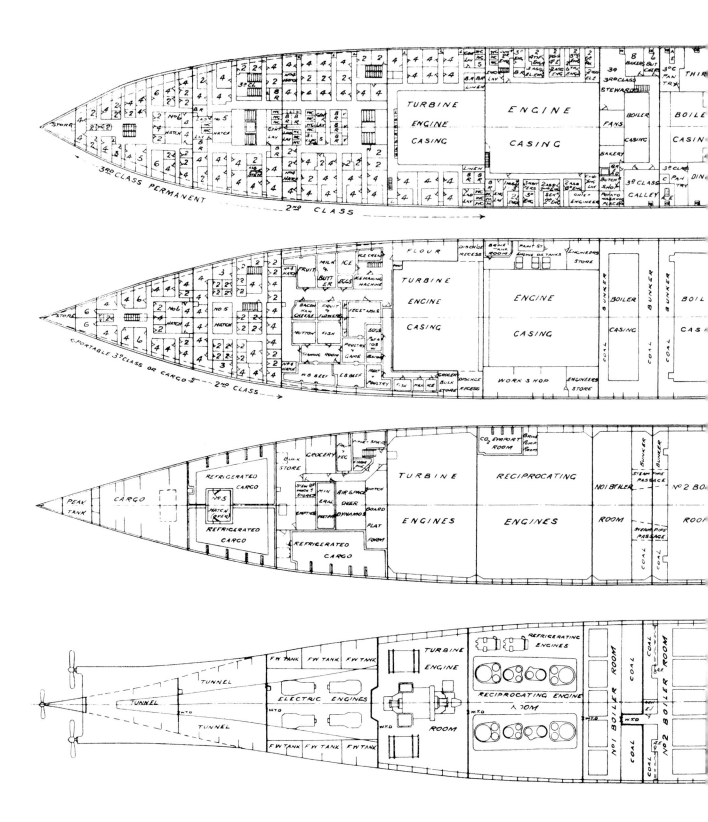

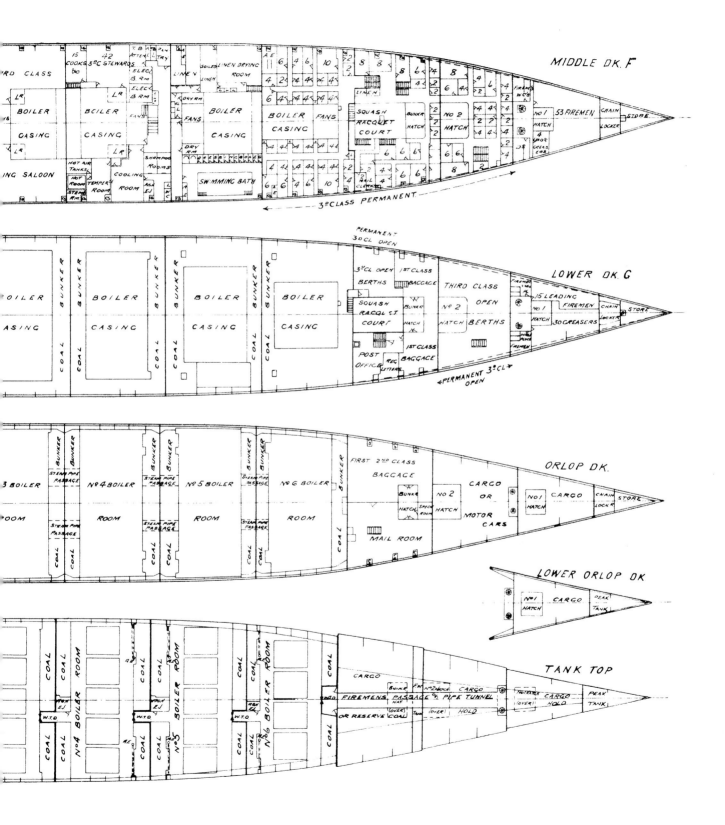

MIDDLE DK. F

RD CLASS

15 42 COOKS 3ºC STEWARDS
T&H
ATTEND PANTRY

LR

BOILER   BOILER
CASING   CASING

LIME V   LINEN

SOILED LINEN DRYING
ROOM

A E   6   4   6   10   7   8   8   6   74   8

LR

LR   LR

DRY RM
FANS

BOILER
CASING

FANS
LINEN

4   2   4   4   4   4   2   6   4   6   4

NO I   53 FIREMEN

CHAIN
STORE

BOILER
CASING

DRY
RM

PRESS'Y   WC   LOCKER

SQUASH
RACQUET
COURT

4   4   4   4   4   4   6   6   6

BUNKR
HATCH

NO 2
HATCH

6   2

FIREMEN
WC'S

NO I
HATCH

4 POT
GREASE'S

4
GREASERS

HOT AIR
TANKS

SHAMPOO
ROOMS

SWIMMING BATH

6   4   6   6   4   4   6   6   8   2

ING SALOON

HOT
ROOM TEMPER'Y
ROOM

COOLING
ROOM

ASA
EJ

STEAM
RM

← 3ºCLASS PERMANENT →

LOWER DK. G

OILER

BUNKER   BUNKER

BOILER
CASING

BUNKER   BUNKER

BOILER
CASING

BUNKER   BUNKER

BOILER
CASING

BUNKER

BOILER
CASING

PERMANENT
3º CL OPEN

3ºCL OPEN   1ST CLASS
BERTHS   BAGGAGE

THIRD CLASS
OPEN
BERTHS

FIREMEN

NO I
HATCH

I/S LEADING
FIREMEN

CHAIN
STORE

ASING   CASING   CASING   CASING

COAL   COAL   COAL   COAL   COAL   COAL   COAL

SQUASH
RACQU'ET
COURT

BUNKR
HATCH

NO 2
HATCH

1ST CLASS
BAGGAGE

30 GREASERS

FIREMEN

4 POT
GREASE

FIREMEN

CHAIN
LOCKER   STORE

POST
OFFICE

REG   BAGGAGE
LETTERS

← PERMANENT 3ºCL →
OPEN

ORLOP DK.

3 BOILER

BUNKER   BUNKER

NO 4 BOILER

STEAM PIPE
PASSAGE

BUNKER   BUNKER

NO 5 BOILER

STEAM PIPE
PASSAGE

BUNKER   BUNKER

NO 6 BOILER

STEAM PIPE
PASSAGE

BUNKER

FIRST 2ND CLASS
BAGGAGE

NO 2
HATCH

CARGO
OR
MOTOR
CARS

NO I
HATCH

CARGO

CHAIN
LOCKER   STORE

ROOM   STEAM PIPE
PASSAGE   ROOM

STEAM PIPE
PASSAGE   ROOM

ROOM

COAL   COAL   COAL   COAL   COAL   COAL   COAL

BUNK'R
HATCH

SPEC'M
ROOM

MAIL ROOM

LOWER ORLOP DK

NO I
HATCH

CARGO

PEAK
TANK

TANK TOP

COAL   COAL

NO 4 BOILER ROOM

COAL   COAL

NO 5 BOILER ROOM

COAL   COAL

NO 6 BOILER ROOM

COAL

CARGO

BUNK'R   FW

NO 2 HATCH   CARGO

MOT TANK

CARGO
HOLD

PEAK
TANK

WTO   ASH
EJ   WTO

ASH
EJ

WTO

AE

FIREMEN'S   PASSAGE & PIPE TUNNEL

OR RESERVE COAL

(OVER)

HAT

(OVER)   HOLD

(OVER)

COAL   COAL   COAL   COAL   COAL   COAL   COAL

Deck construction

All decks on the Olympic Class were of steel. Within the ship girder the deck-supporting beams were of channel bar, 10in deep with 3in flanges, with a maximum breadth of 92ft. The beams were plated over to form the decks, with thicker plates being used on the Bridge and Shelter Decks (as well as on the sheer strakes) with doubling (two thicknesses of plating) at points where high stresses were to be expected, such as at the outer strakes (stringers) of the deck plating.

Above the ship girder the beams were of a lighter section channel, generally 6in with 2½in flanges, as was the deck plating, to both reduce weight and lower the centre of gravity. Two expansion joints were incorporated in these upper superstructures to take up any movement caused by longitudinal flexing of the ship's hull in heavy weather.

The beams, connected to the frames by brackets ('knees'), had camber, or round-of-beam. This was a transverse curvature extending outwards and downwards. It was incorporated to assist in drainage of the decks and was, at the centreline, 3in higher than at the sides. Beams were connected to each other with pillars.

Externally, the decks exposed to the weather were planked with 5in x 3in section yellow pine and caulked, while internally the decks were either covered with Harding's 'Litosilo' (40,000sq yd were used) before carpets were laid or in 'wet' areas, such as washrooms, toilets and the Turkish Bath, with ceramic tiles embedded in Portland cement.

RIGHT Deck planking on the tug-tender *Calshot* at Southampton. *(Authors' Collections)*

RIGHT The bedroom of First Class suite B60 opened into its own drawing room. This suite would be occupied by Quigg Baxter, age 24, from Montreal, with his mother, Mrs James Baxter, and sister, Suzette Douglas, during the maiden voyage. The two women were rescued in Lifeboat No. 6, but Mr Baxter did not survive the sinking. *(UFTM H1726)*

Passenger accommodation

The *Titanic* could accommodate 739 First Class, 674 Second Class and 1,026 Third Class passengers. In addition, she had a crew of about 900 and was capable of carrying some 3,339 persons in total.

Old-style liners had been decorated in the manner of baronial halls and country mansions. In contrast, the public rooms of the *Titanic* and *Olympic* reflected the lighter style of contemporary hotels much favoured by American travellers. First Class cabins were sumptuously finished in regal and Empire styles.

ABOVE The Smoke Room of the *Olympic*. The mahogany panelling was inlaid with mother-of-pearl and the stained-glass panelled structure (illuminated from the other side to give an impression of daylight) concealed a funnel uptake. *(UFTM H1549)*

RIGHT The Café Parisian, unique at the time to the *Titanic*, covered what was part of the Second Class promenade deck on the *Olympic*. The adjacent à la carte restaurant was similarly extended out to the port side of the ship. *(UFTM H1733)*

ABOVE One of the large alcove rooms that winged the First Class Dining Saloon. *(UFTM H1545)*

LEFT Part of the Grand Stairway that descended through five decks from the Boat Deck down to the Dining Saloon Reception Room on Saloon Deck 'D'. *(UFTM H1597)*

BELOW The Grand Stairway at its lower end made a spectacular entrance to the Reception Room. A carved clock case depicting 'Honour and Glory Crowning Time' graced the landing. *(Titanic International)*

RIGHT The sumptuously carved and decorated Louis-Quinze First Class Lounge on Promenade Deck 'A' reflected White Star's desire to decorate its big ships in the style of the Ritz Hotel rather than the baronial styles of other lines, the former appealing more to American taste. *(UFTM H1547)*

BELOW A typical Third Class cabin decorated in plain white enamelled panelling. Counterpanes woven with the White Star motif discouraged pilferage. *(UFTM H1796)*

BELOW The Plunge Bath was one of the earliest swimming pools afloat, the first having been installed on the *Adriatic*. *(Authors' Collections)*

LEFT The gymnasium on the Boat Deck gave First Class passengers the opportunity to work off those pounds gained in the Dining Saloon. *(Cork Examiner)*

Lifeboats

The *Titanic* was equipped with 20 lifeboats of 4 different designs, the number exceeding the existing Board of Trade requirements. The lifeboats were of wooden construction (although the collapsible boats had folding canvas sides) and were designed to take more than their intended capacity in weight (see Chapter 4).

Davits

Mechanical arms, known as davits, lifted and lowered loaded lifeboats into the water. Lifeboats had to be classed as being 'under davits' (within reach of the davits) to be effective, thus rendering almost useless two collapsibles stowed on the roof of the officers' quarters (see Chapter 4).

Engines

The *Titanic* was a triple-screw steamer driven by a combination of reciprocating engines with a Parsons low-pressure turbine. Each wing propeller was driven by one set of reciprocating engines, and the central propeller by the low pressure turbine. (For a fuller description of the *Titanic*'s propulsion machinery and associated equipment, see Chapter 3.)

Funnels

The *Titanic* and her two sisters had four distinguishable and elegant funnels, of which the three forward ones took the smoke from the boilers, up to 20 spider-like boiler exhaust flues being allocated to each funnel for this purpose. The fourth, aftermost 'dummy' funnel on the Olympic Class was used for ventilation purposes and taking exhaust fumes from various galleys, engine rooms, and the fireplace in the First Class Smoke Room.

When the *Olympic* was converted to an oil-fired ship in the early 1920s, a fan was installed to extract the flammable gases that escaped from the oil storage tanks. Ladders fitted inside the dummy funnel gave access to the various fittings and trunking so that they were easily reached by the ship's engineers for cleaning and maintenance.

RIGHT The *Britannic*'s 'dummy' fourth funnel being hoisted into a vertical position by a floating crane. This was then lifted into place while the ship was in the outfitting dock. *(UFTM H1993)*

OPPOSITE On the Olympic Class the aftermost of the four funnels was a 'dummy' and was not used for carrying away the products of combustion. Its chief function was to ventilate the engine rooms and the galleys. The galley flues from the ovens also passed up this funnel and through another pipe which led to the top of the funnel. *(Authors' Collections)*

RIGHT The *Olympic*'s giant spider-like exhaust uptakes nearing completion at Harland & Wolff's works. These uptakes carried the combustion gases (and soot) to the three funnels and accounted for the massive internal space needed above the boiler rooms. *(UFTM H2381)*

black top (so painted to help disguise soot marks around the crown of the funnels) was just over one-quarter of the depth of the funnel. At the time, the number of funnels on a ship was taken by the travelling public and publicists to be indicative of power – and ultimately, but erroneously, safety.

Propellers

As far back as 1872 Harland & Wolff and the White Star Line had settled on prefabricated propellers whereby cast-iron blades were originally bolted on to the cast-iron propeller boss rather than the more popular fully cast-iron (or later bronze) screw. In this manner it was cheaper in material and labour costs for repairs to lose an occasional blade and have a new one bolted on rather than wreck a complete cast propeller. Also, with the vessels of White Star having the same size propellers, the bolt-on blades could be interchangeable and spares readily made and stored in Liverpool and Belfast to be used on different ships. Closely related metals such as cast iron, wrought iron and, later, steel were compatible, but with the introduction of bronze blades bolted on to cast steel bosses another factor crept in. Although steel and bronze were stronger metals, their close contact in the presence of sea water introduced the onset

ABOVE A sunny but almost deserted Boat Deck and flying flags show that this was *Titanic* in Southampton on Good Friday, 1912, the only time that the liner was dressed overall. *(Authors' Collections)*

The funnels had an elliptical cross-section of 24ft 6in by 19ft, were just over 70ft high above the Boat Deck, and were raked aft to about 11 degrees. The tops of the funnels were 150ft above the furnace bars.

Each funnel was supported by six stays of wound wire rope cable attached to lugs on a strengthening ring located at the base of the black-painted funnel-top. The funnel itself was painted in the White Star livery of buff, and the

RIGHT The after propeller brackets. This major component was built up of a central cast section plate on to which were bolted the cast steel propeller boss supports. The whole structure weighed nearly 74 tons. The assembly is seen here in the workshop mounted on a lathe or a jig-borer before finish-machining the centre aperture to take the central shaft. *(The Shipbuilder)*

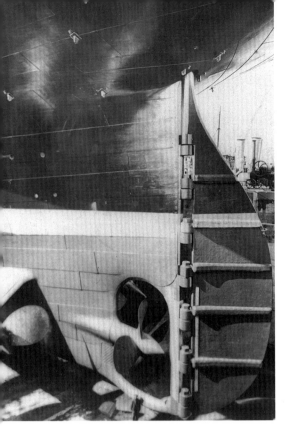

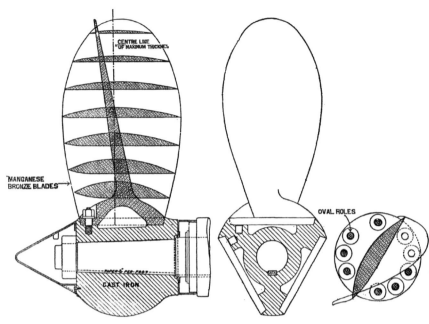

ABOVE The stern section with rudder and propellers. Note the intricate and complex shape of the plating surrounding the port wing propeller shaft. Note also the lugs positioned under the counter stern. These were strategically riveted in place to frames during construction and served to sling propellers and blading during build and removal. The man in the picture gives some idea of the sheer size of components used. *(US Library of Congress)*

ABOVE An illustration of a typical three-bladed propeller as used by merchant ships of the era. The *Titanic*'s hubs, or bosses, were in fact manufactured from cast steel. This material was stronger and tougher than cast iron as identified in the illustration. Also, each blade was secured to its root by eight nuts and studs. *(Authors' Collections)*

BELOW *Olympic*'s outer wing propeller bosses and centre propeller on the quayside before fitting. At the top of the right-hand boss can be seen the keyway (slot) machined for its location on its shaft. The location land for the bronze blade root may be clearly seen. In the background is the floating crane. *(UFTM H1510)*

of electrolytic or galvanic corrosion. Over a period of time the nuts and studs corroded and a blade would shed. Regular dry-docking and maintenance during refit ensured the propeller's condition was checked, and if necessary, changed. This problem would later be overcome by using bronze bosses with detachable bronze blades.

Early damage to the *Olympic*'s propellers in September 1911 and February 1912 necessitated her return to Belfast for repairs. In the case of a loss or a very badly damaged blade it could replaced by undoing the bronze nuts from the studs attaching the blade and fitting a spare blade. In the era when welding was in its infancy, small chunks lost from a propeller blade, or scoring, could be repaired by either 'dressing off' (filing smooth and buffing to

time the large round 'collar' type nuts were fitted in place to protect their threads.

The *Titanic* was initially dry-docked in the Thompson Graving Dock and the dock emptied. The two 38-ton wing propellers and the 22-ton centre propeller were brought from their storage area by the 200-ton-lift floating crane and deposited on the floor of the dry dock near the ship's stern. Scaffolding was then erected around the area of the tail shafts, giving room for the propellers to be manoeuvred into place. Before fitting, the protective nuts were removed, the canvas and tallow sheathing removed, and the machined surfaces cleaned up.

Using the 13 large lugs that were provided for shackles that were built into the frames under the *Titanic*'s counter stern and a combination of the four pairs of bollards on her Poop Deck, in addition to the odd bollard on the dockside, these anchor points were used to sling the block and tackles that would fit or remove the *Titanic*'s propellers.

It is likely that the centre four-bladed propeller was fitted first, being more awkward to manoeuvre between the stern frame and rudder pintles. The end of the propeller shaft, like the propeller bore, was tapered, and in the bore of the propeller a keyway was cut in the form of a straight parallel groove with a corresponding one in the shaft. The shaft was positioned so that the keyway was at the top, dead centre, and into the groove on the shaft

Fitting a propeller

The task of changing and fitting a propeller was a massive undertaking that required the ship to be dry-docked.

The tail shafting and associated tunnel bearings were installed in the stern tube while the ship was on the slip before launching. Protective sheathing in the form of canvas and tallow grease may well have been wrapped around the machined tapered lengths that protruded from the stern tubes. At the same

a mild steel key or 'feather' was placed, and the tail shaft greased accordingly.

The centre propeller was slung by chains looped around two of its blades near the hub, with its keyway uppermost and the larger bore of its taper facing the tail shaft. With the centre propeller lifted by a combination of slings, strops and block and tackles from both sides of the stern, to signals and commands from the foreman, the propeller was eased slowly into the vertical position and coaxed in such a way that it was offered up to the tapered shaft. Using the combination of the pulley blocks and manpower gently ramming the hub with railway sleepers, the propeller was pushed home on its mating tapered tail shaft.

As the centre propeller rotated clockwise, looking from astern, a large left-handed collar nut was handled by two men on to its respective male thread and screwed up as far as it would go by hand. In order to ensure it was tightened home, either a 'tommy' bar was inserted in the holes in the nut's outer circumference and 'barred' around (in a similar manner to an old sailing ship capstan), or a snug-fitting 'C' spanner was used with a peg that located in the holes and a long handle for leverage. If necessary, the fitters would flog the spanner handle with sledgehammers until the nut was fastened up and the propeller boss was hard up against its locating spigot on the tail shaft. The nut was probably secured from working loose by a cottar pin inserted through a hole drilled through the shaft in line with one set of diametrically opposed holes to prevent it working back. Over the nut a steel conical fairing was secured to protect the nuts and threads. This reduced the loss by eddying motion of the water and prevented fouling of the ropes.

The two outboard propellers could be built up by first fitting the boss and then bolting on each blade. The slinging of them by pulleys was less complicated, but safety slings were still required to the Poop Deck bollards. As the wing propellers of the *Titanic* were outward turning, the tail-shaft thread and nut was left-handed on the starboard propeller and right-handed for the port propeller. In this manner the propellers were kept hard up when the shafts were rotating under normal ahead conditions.

ABOVE *Titanic*'s starboard tail shaft is fitted just before her launch. Note that the rudder has been secured by braces in order to keep it in the amidships position during the launch. The man on the shaft's end is sitting on the shaft taper and leaning over the propeller boss, securing the nut. This nut, which has to be put into place to protect the threads, is of a round collar-type with about six holes in it so the nut might be tightened with a 'tommy bar' or a 'C' spanner. Halfway along the shaft may be seen the bowler hat of the foreman in charge of the gang, standing behind the shaft. *(UFTM H1857)*

BELOW The *Olympic*'s centre propeller slung by chains. Note the larger bore of the taper nearer the camera and the shaft's keyway slot at the 10 o'clock position. *(UFTM H1457)*

remove sharp edges), or casting, in which case molten bronze would be poured into a box built around the blade to make up the loss; this was then dressed off. An alternative method known as 'hammer welding', which was used on smaller propellers, may also have been used. As previously mentioned, a blade might shed in time due to electrolytic/galvanic corrosion in which the cast steel hub became a huge sacrificial anode and weakened in the area where the studs were located.

Rudder and steering engines

The *Titanic*'s massive bulk was steered by a solid cast steel 'plate' rudder made up of six sections bolted together, with an overall height of 78ft 8in and length of 15ft 3in. It weighed 101¼ tons, which meant that no steering arrangement reliant on manual power alone, regardless of how much leverage was in the system, would have been strong enough to move it. To solve this problem, an enormous steering gear and two engines were installed in the poop at the after end of the shelter deck. The whole unit was of the Wilson-Pirrie type, manufactured by Harland & Wolff, and each engine was powered by the ship's steam supply under pressure from the boilers, with cylinders much like those in the main reciprocating engines.

The steering gear itself was driven by one of the two steering engines. It consisted of a large spring quadrant and tiller on the rudder head operated via rack-and-pinion and bevel gearing. Although *Titanic* had two steering engines, one mounted either side of the ship's centreline, only one was used at any given time, the other being kept as a standby.

The large quadrant was connected to the arms of the working tiller by heavy spring links, which prevented undue shocks being experienced by the gear or the engine. The working tiller consisted of two forged arms, one arm of which was placed at the centre of each half of the quadrant. The tiller arms were keyed to the rudder head, and were tied together by a strong wrought steel tie-bar. A spare tiller was situated on top of the quadrant and

ABOVE The *Britannic*'s steering engine in the workshop. The two large arc covers at the engine's centre house the two spur-and-bevel gearings necessary to mesh with gear teeth on the rudder quadrant. *(UFTM H1976)*

BELOW The Poop deck and after Well Deck were the promenade deck areas for Third Class passengers, along with their associated cranes and cargo hatch. Note the Docking Bridge in the background, with its telegraphs and wheel for direct connection to the steering gear and after-conning operations. *(Cork Examiner)*

BELOW A functional diagram to show how the rudder quadrant is operated. The Olympic Class were worked by spur-and-bevel gearing rather than the worm-and-wheel mechanism shown.
(Authors' Collections)

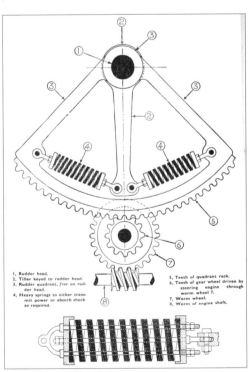

1, Rudder head.
2, Tiller keyed to rudder head.
3, Rudder quadrant, *free on rudder head.*
4, Heavy springs to either transmit power or absorb shock as required.

5, Teeth of quadrant rack.
6, Teeth of gear wheel driven by steering engine through worm wheel 7.
7, Worm wheel.
8, Worm of engine shaft.

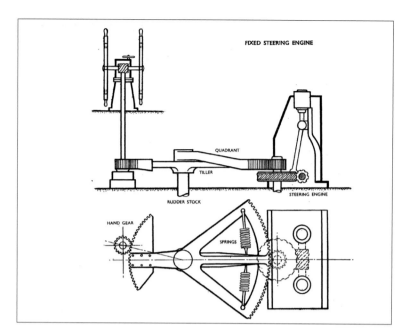

was operated in the case of the quadrant and working tiller being disabled. This spare tiller could also be worked by the warping capstans if the whole gear failed.

Anchors, capstans and windlasses

There were five anchors on the Olympic Class: one port and one starboard, stowed in hawsepipes, aft of the stem, each weighing 7¾ tons; a third (15½ tons) stowed on deck at the prow at the forecastle on the centreline; and two Kedging anchors.

The two side anchors were raised and lowered using chain cable. The anchor cables were made up in links or shackles of 12½

ABOVE A simplified diagram of a fixed steering engine showing the after-conning gearwheels engaged, whereby in an emergency the ship could be steered from the Docking Bridge.
(Authors' Collections)

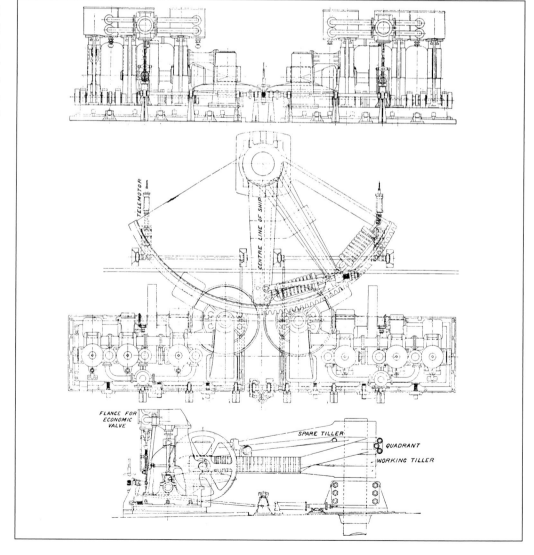

RIGHT Wilson-Pirrie type steering gear as used on the *Titanic*.
(The Shipbuilder)

ABOVE *Olympic*'s foredeck showing the stowed bow anchor in foreground on its cradle, anchor chains and hawsepipes for the central (bow), port and starboard anchors, foremast, and in the background the ship's bridge superstructure. *(UFTM H1826)*

ABOVE *Titanic*'s port bower anchor is well illustrated in this photograph in a partially lowered state while the liner was in the Thompson Dock. The chimney to the dock's Pump House boiler room can be seen to the left. *(UFTM H1515)*

BELOW The shipboard end of the anchor chain was secured to a chain-locker bulkhead by a chain plate. The floor of the chain locker was cemented at an angle towards a drain and covered with timber slats to allow drainage from the wet and muddy cables. *(Authors' Collections)*

BELOW A sketch showing an anchor housed in its hawsepipe. *(Authors' Collections)*

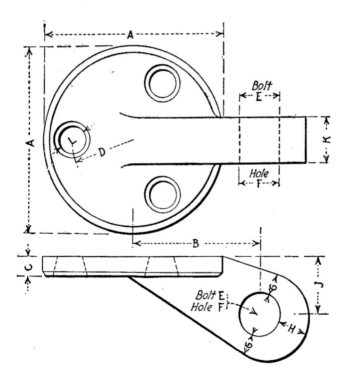

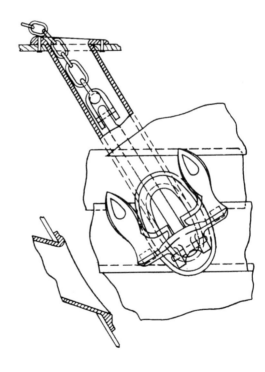

RIGHT Like the anchor chains, *Titanic*'s 15½-ton bow (or centre) anchor was made at Noah Hingley's ironworks at Netherton. The ship had three anchors that weighed a total of 31 tons. The anchor, painted white for display and emblazoned with the maker's name, was hauled 'in state' through the town by a large team of shire horses. *(Authors' Collections)*

Anchors and chains

BELOW Anchor chain-making at Noah Hingley & Sons' ironworks at Netherton in the Midlands, in 1911. This is Ben Hodgetts' chain gang. From left to right: Ben Woodhouse, George Bridgwater, Albert Hodgetts, Theophilus Dunn, Ben Hodgetts. *(Authors' Collections)*

Titanic's bow (or centre) anchor and 93 tons of forged chain links were manufactured at Netherton, near Dudley – 'anchor-making capital of the world' – before being shipped from Fleetwood in Lancashire across the Irish Sea to Harland & Wolff's shipyard in Belfast.

Anchors

In 1911, *Titanic*'s 15½-ton bow anchor – a variant on the Hall's improved stockless type (the design of which had been sanctioned by Lloyd's of London on 5 May 1910), but having a square-sectioned shank in lieu of a

round – was at the time, along with that of the *Olympic*, the largest ever forged. The ship had three anchors that weighed a total of 31 tons, the prime contractor being Noah Hingley & Sons of Netherton in the Black Country, which subcontracted some of its manufacturing to other ironworks.

Hingley's manufactured the anchor shackle and pin, anchor head locking pins and retaining blocks, anchor attachment links, anchor chains (for the two side anchors), mooring swivel chains and anchor chains deck-stoppers for *Titanic*. Casting of the anchor head was by John Rogerson & Co of Newcastle upon Tyne, and the steel hand and drop-forged anchor shank were subcontracted to Walter Somers Ltd in Halesowen. The constituent parts were then assembled at Netherton. The 175 fathoms of steel wire cable for the centre anchor, with a circumference of 9½in, was manufactured by Messrs Bullivant & Co of London.

The head of the anchor was cast in a sand mould formed by impressing full-scale wooden moulds of the anchor head sections into the sand. Molten metal was then poured into the mould and, when it was cool, the casting was raised from the sand mould and any superfluous attachments chipped off.

The anchor shank was forged into shape by steam-driven drop forge hammers. The end product was an object over 15ft long and weighing almost 8 tons. The eyelets at both ends of the shank, through which the securing pins would be passed to secure the head and shackle, were forged into the shank during its manufacture. Once the desired shape was achieved, the eyelets were cleaned up.

The anchor parts were then subjected to proofing at the nearby Lloyd's Proving House. Included in the schedule was the drop test when the assembled anchor was raised to a height of 12ft and dropped on to a solid concrete, steel-topped floor. This process was to establish the drop-load of the anchor when at sea.

Next, the anchor was hammer-tested: in a raised position, its head and shank were struck with a hammer. If this test produced a clear ringing sound it indicated a soundness of casting. The anchor, being proved to have no imperfections, was passed as fit for purpose.

Anchor chains

Some 1,200ft of forged chain links, each link weighing 175lb, were made for *Titanic* at the Hingley Works. Each link was forged from pig-iron bars that were heated and run through a machine known as a mandrel, which gave the link its distinctive oval shape, although its ends were not yet closed up. The link was next heated in a furnace while a centre stud was hammered into place and the link was then hooped into its neighbouring closed-up link. Then the chain gang would close the link and fuse the ends together by hammer welding.

Lengths of chain cable were tested at the Hingley Works in hydraulic pulling beds. One end of a length of chain was attached to a stationary clamp while the other end was fitted into the jaws of the testing machine. Pressure was then applied to the chains to pulls specified by Lloyd's.

fathoms length, each link having a diameter of 3½in. Each cable was 165 fathoms in length, weighed 48 tons and was raised and lowered using two capstans with operating machinery placed on the deck beneath (Shelter Deck C).

The Foredeck was protected from damage as the chains passed aft from the hawsepipes before turning inboard around the capstans. They were guided below through pipes (extending down to the locker through trimmers' and firemen's messes, a sleep-preventing operation when cable was being paid out or heaved) to the deep Chain Locker located between the Orlop Deck and Middle Deck F. The inboard end of the chain was attached to a heavy lug, a chain plate, on the locker floor. This perforated floor, raised above the actual deck, allowed residue mud and water to drain off the chain.

The 15½-ton anchor was stowed in a well at the fore end of the Foredeck and forward of the hawsepipes' upper accesses. This large anchor was manipulated using a dedicated derrick that had its seating on the Shelter Deck below, and was raised and lowered using a wound wire cable of 9½in circumference and 175 fathoms in length, operated by a windlass and stowed around a large grooved drum located on the Shelter Deck. The wire cable was paid out through a hawsepipe cast into the upper stem and was also used when towing from ahead.

Kedging anchors, one sited starboard on the Foredeck, the other on the Poop Deck, were a smaller type of anchor for use when 'kedging' the ship. They would be lowered overboard, taken some distance from the ship and used to 'drag' the ship to a new position. They had a rigid stock and a head pivoted about the shank.

Two sets of capstans were sited on both Foredeck and Poop and took mooring lines from the bollards.

Electric plant

The homes of most Britons in 1912 were still lit by gas or oil lamps, while coal was widely used for cooking and heating. In contrast, the *Titanic* was a marvel of the age because she used electricity extensively in all her departments on board. Over 200 miles of cabling delivered electricity throughout the ship for lighting and heating, and to provide electrical power for hundreds of different types of machinery, ranging from deck cranes to potato peelers, and from watertight door operation to stoking indicators. Her four massive 400kW electrical generators produced more power than a typical large city power station of the day.

Refrigeration

The ship's refrigeration plant was supplied by two horizontal duplex CO_2 machines, which provided four separate refrigeration units. These machines were situated on the port side of the reciprocating engine room at floor level. The plant refrigerated and cooled the ship's extensive provision rooms on the Lower and Orlop Decks, as well as a number of cold larders in the bars and pantries in different parts of the ship, and supplied refrigeration for ice making and cooled drinking water in the First, Second and Third Class accommodation.

Olympic Class waterworks

An enormous amount of fresh water was needed during a voyage on the *Titanic*. Although she could distil fresh water from sea water during the journey, the main water supply was taken aboard while the ship was in Southampton and stored in the ship's double-bottom tanks. Hot and cold water were carried to all parts of the ship through a complicated system of pipes, pumps and valves. The *Titanic* also had its own distilling plant, so that at any time and in an emergency fresh water could be distilled from the sea. This method was a costly process, as it involved constant cleaning and repair owing to the clogging of salts from the sea water which impaired the efficiency of the distillation plant.

Ventilation

Over the Reciprocating Engine Room was a light and air shaft which extended above the boat deck and was surmounted by a large skylight. The similar shaft from the Turbine Room was surmounted by the fourth ('dummy') funnel. Ventilation of the Engine Room was further assisted by four electrically driven 'Sirocco' extractor fans.

Ventilation and heating of passenger accommodation was by means of warm air driven by electric fans, which was distributed to cabins, staterooms and passageways via insulated trunking. Each First Class room was also fitted with an electric heater for passengers who required additional warmth.

Extractor fans were fitted in lavatories, galleys, pantries and other quarters for the removal of noxious odours.

Natural ventilation was provided by some 2,000 windows and sidelights, the largest of which were in the public rooms on the Bridge, Promenade and Boat Decks, and in the gymnasium.

Radio and navigational aids

The wireless telegraphy installation on the *Titanic* consisted of a Marconi 1½kW standard ship's set, situated in the radio room on the Bridge Deck. The two parallel wires required for the system extended between the two main masts and were kept as high as possible, and at least 50ft above the tops of the funnels. From the aerial wires, connecting wires led down to the instruments in the Radio Room. There were two complete sets of apparatus – one for transmitting and one for receiving messages, the latter being placed in a sound-proofed booth built in the corner of the room.

The *Titanic* was equipped with two magnetic compasses on the Captain's bridge, with an additional instrument on the Docking Bridge aft. A standard compass was also provided. It was situated on a brass compass platform on the boat deck, 12ft away from any iron or steel that might affect its reading.

Two electrically driven depth-sounding machines were installed on spars adjacent to the bridge, enabling depth soundings to be taken when the ship was underway.

OPPOSITE On the left-hand side of the picture, only the cold fresh water system is shown, and on the right-hand side the hot water system; both systems were fitted in all parts of the ship.
(Authors' Collections)

Chapter Three

Propulsion

Triple screws driven by
a combination of steam
reciprocating and low-pressure
turbine engines powered the
Titanic. Steam for her huge
engines was generated by
29 boilers (of which 24 were
double-ended) fed by 159
furnaces, which consumed around
850 tons of coal per day.

**Stern view of all three propellers on the *Olympic*, seen from the
dry-dock floor.** *(UFTM H1796)*

ABOVE Two rows of almost complete boilers for the *Olympic* in Harland & Wolff's Boiler Shop. These were built by the firm's workforce of boilermakers, a now extinct trade. The figure between the rows gives some idea of the scale. *(UFTM H1455)*

RIGHT Cutaway profile view of *Titanic* showing the location of her power plant and associated equipment. *(Getty Images)*

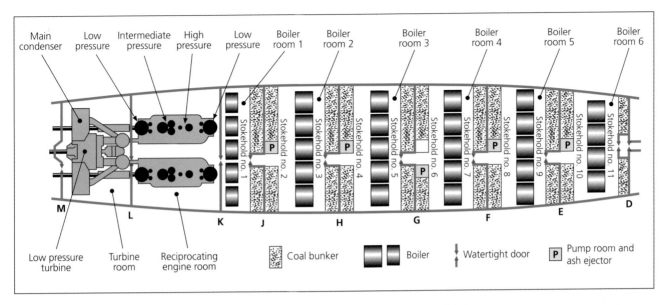

Main condenser — Low pressure — Intermediate pressure — High pressure — Low pressure — Boiler room 1 — Boiler room 2 — Boiler room 3 — Boiler room 4 — Boiler room 5 — Boiler room 6

Stokehold no. 1 · Stokehold no. 2 · Stokehold no. 3 · Stokehold no. 4 · Stokehold no. 5 · Stokehold no. 6 · Stokehold no. 7 · Stokehold no. 8 · Stokehold no. 9 · Stokehold no. 10 · Stokehold no. 11

M   L   K   J   H   G   F   E   D

Low pressure turbine — Turbine room — Reciprocating engine room

Coal bunker   Boiler   Watertight door   P Pump room and ash ejector

In a ship so large for its day, the *Titanic* (and her sister the *Olympic*) was driven by a combination of steam reciprocating engines and a turbine located in the two lowermost decks, Orlop and Tank Top. These were overseen by a staff of 22 engineers and 6 electricians.

In these vast external combustion engines coal was burned to generate steam in the boilers. The 'live' steam at high pressure was in turn used to expand through the three-stage cylinders of the engines and converted the heat energy to mechanical energy, which in turn powered the ship's outer propellers.

The expanded energy at this stage could not be used in a reciprocating engine proper because of cylinder size limitations. The combination of reciprocating engines together with a Parsons LP turbine was first introduced by Harland & Wolff on White Star's *Laurentic* of 1909. The system offered superior economy with an increase in power, all for the same steam consumption. These benefits were

ABOVE Internal arrangement of *Titanic*'s power plant. *(Matthew Marke)*

Titanic's boilers

No of double-ended boilers	24
No of single-ended boilers	5
Diameter of all boilers	15ft 9in
Length of double-ended boilers	21ft
Length of single-ended boilers	11ft 9in
No of furnaces on each double-ended boiler	6
No of furnaces on each single-ended boiler	3
Total heating surface per double-ended boiler	5,702sq ft
Total grate area per double-ended boiler	130.8sq ft
Total heating surface per single-ended boiler	2,822sq ft
Total grate area per single-ended boiler	65.4sq ft
Ratio of heating surface to grate surface	43:1
Inside diameter of furnace corrugations	3ft 9in
Type of corrugation	Morison
Total no of furnaces	159
Boiler working pressure	215psi (gauge)
Test pressure	430psi (gauge)

achieved by further expanding the exhaust steam at a much greater volume from the reciprocating machinery in the LP turbine, beyond the limits that were possible with the reciprocating engine.

The trials and operating experience of the *Laurentic* led to Harland & Wolff adopting the combination machinery for the Olympic Class trio.

In the 'open feed system', as it was known, after passing through the Parsons turbine the now 'spent' or 'dead' steam entered the condenser where it was effectively condensed back into water to be used in the cycle again.

Scotch boilers

Steam for the *Titanic*'s engines was generated in 24 double-ended and 5 single-ended cylindrical or 'Scotch' boilers under natural draught conditions. Each double-ended boiler contained 6 furnaces (3 at each end) while each single-ended contained 3.

In this type of boiler combustion took place in the furnaces which were, as far as possible, surrounded by water. Tubes, also surrounded by water, took the products of combustion away from the furnaces and from the combustion space while dissipating the heat from the gases into the water. Of necessity, the pressure vessel was of a large diameter because the furnaces and combustion chamber

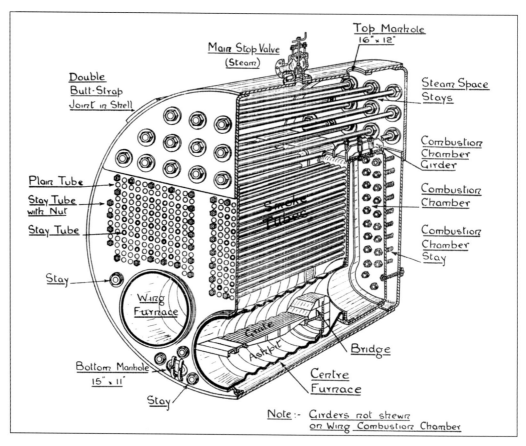

RIGHT Cutaway drawing of a single-ended Scotch boiler showing the main parts used in its construction.
(Authors' Collections)

were contained within the water space. The Scotch marine boiler was constructed of rolled mild steel plate $1\frac{43}{64}$in thick with an ultimate tensile strength (UTS) of 28–32 tons/in².

The shells of the single-ended boilers were formed in a single ring and those of the double-ended in three rings (each in two halves), joined by two treble-riveted double-butt strap joints. Each double-ended boiler was 15ft 9in in diameter and 21ft long, while the single-ended boilers were 11ft 9in long. Inside the shell were three corrugated furnaces riveted at one end to a rectangular shaped combustion chamber. Three nests containing a total of 430 fire (or smoke) tubes connected the combustion chamber to the boiler front. Water surrounded the whole of the furnaces, combustion chamber and tubes. All flat surfaces were reinforced between the end plates by 18 longitudinal stays of 3in and 3¼in diameter, and were secured by nuts on either side of the plates. Similar stays supported the bottom of the end plates, and usually there were two stays around each manhole. The plain tubes were expanded into the tube plate, with 256 of the tubes being thick-walled stay tubes screwed into

both tube plates and 106 of them secured with a nut at one end.

The combustion chamber walls were supported by smaller stays of around 1¾in

ABOVE Triple-furnace boilers destined for the *Britannic* in Harland & Wolff's Boiler Shop. Note below the boiler nearest the camera, a stack of fire tubes and just beside them some boiler stays which support the boiler internally. (UFTM H1939)

LEFT One of *Britannic*'s boilers ready for installation while she was alongside at the outfitting dock. (UFTM H1967)

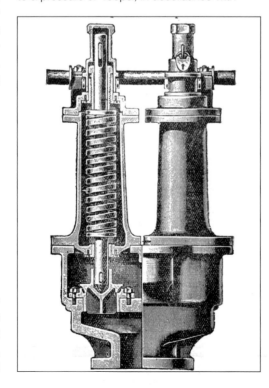

diameter at 7⅜in intervals. The combustion chamber top was supported by the chamber's walls, girders and stays.

The furnaces were made from 'Morison' pattern corrugated steel which gave an increased heating surface area. They were of 3ft 9in diameter and fitted with fronts of the Downie 'boltless' pattern. The boilers' working pressure was 215psi but they were hydraulically tested to a pressure of 430psi, in accordance with Board of Trade regulations. Essential mountings included:

Two safety valves on top of the shell These valves automatically opened when the boiler pressure exceeded the normal (*i.e.* 215psi) and allowed the steam to escape up the waste steam pipe on the funnel.

Main steam stop valve This valve was fitted to the top of each boiler and controlled the supply of steam to the main engines.

Main feed check valve The feed water returning from the engines entered the boiler through this valve, admitted water just below the working water level, replenishing the water as steam was formed.

Auxiliary feed check valve Standby valve in case of an accident to the other.

Two water gauges One was fitted to each side of the boiler to average the height indication during the ship's rolling. The water gauge determined the level of water inside the boiler.

Steam pressure gauge Each boiler was fitted with a brass 'Bordon tube' pressure gauge which indicated the pressure of steam generated. A small sector on the gauge's white dial was painted red to indicate the maximum working pressure of the boiler (dubbed 'the blood' by firemen).

Salinometer cock This was used to draw off a sample of the boiler water for test purposes, especially for salt content.

Scum valve These were fitted to the boiler shell with an internal pipe terminating in a pan (or dish) at the end, which was just below the boiler water level. They were used to cleanse the surface of the water from oil or other floating impurities.

Blow down valve This was used to blow out mud and scale and other heavy impurities and also to reduce the water level as required. It was situated near the bottom of the boiler and connected to a valve in the ship's side. The steam pressure in the boiler was used to blow the water out to sea through this valve.

Circulating valve The valve was fitted to the boiler near its bottom and was used only to produce an artificial circulation of the water when raising steam. This minimised stresses produced during unequal expansion of the boiler plates and aided more effective heat

transfer to the water. Ross-Schofield boiler circulators were used on the *Titanic*.

Manholes There was always one manhole on the boiler shell at the top, to give access to the inside of the boiler above the furnaces, and one between each pair of furnaces. The holes were elliptical in shape and were closed by an elliptical door held in place by nuts and brass stays (dogs) outside the boiler.

Raising steam

When lighting a Scotch boiler, the boiler was first filled with clean fresh water to a level indicated by three-quarters of the gauge glass, as this allowed for losses that may have occurred while warming through. Water was originally supplied by means of a hose from a shoreside jetty or a water barge alongside.

The fire was usually lit in the centre furnace first. Kindling wood and rags soaked in paraffin oil were placed on the furnace grate and covered with coal to a depth of 4–6in. With the boiler dampers open and the main steam stop valve shut, the rags and wood were set alight and when well under way the fire would soon spread across the whole grate. The two

adjacent furnaces were lit by a shovelful of red-hot coals.

Heating the water to boiling point and turning it into steam took 18–24 hours, therefore 24 hours' notice was generally given to engineers before steam was available to turn the engines. Since heat from the furnaces rose, the water above the furnaces became heated while water below the furnaces and near the boiler bottom heated less readily and artificial circulation by the boiler circulators was resorted to. A steam-driven feed pump was started using steam from a small auxiliary or 'donkey' boiler. The pump drew water out of the boiler through the circulating valve and returned it to the top part of the boiler through the auxiliary feed check valve, thus allowing the heated water above the furnaces to fall to the bottom and heat this part uniformly. When steam was generated this artificial circulation was stopped and the steam pressure was then generally raised to the normal working pressure of 215psi.

Firemen

The *Titanic*'s 24 double-ended boilers were labour intensive and for each 4-hour watch there were 48 firemen, 20 trimmers and 5 leading firemen on duty. Each boiler room required 4 trimmers to cart the coal and carry ash to the ejectors, mainly because there were 2 stokeholds in each of these rooms, 1 forward and 1 aft, and each stokehold in turn had 2 bunkers – 1 to port and the other to starboard. To feed the boiler furnaces needed from 8 to 10 firemen. One fireman was responsible for working one end of a double-ended boiler. Leading firemen supervised the personnel in the double-ended boiler rooms.

The duties of the firemen were to keep the supply of coal to the furnaces and to maintain the rapid steam supply.

Stoking

To help harmonise the firemen's duty a device known as Kilroy's Stoking Regulator, in conjunction with Kilroy's Stoking Indicator, was employed. The stoking regulator could be set to regulate the firing of the furnaces every 8, 9, 10, 12, 15, 20, 25 or 30 minutes, depending upon how much steam was needed and the number of boilers that were on stream at any time. The

BELOW A Scotch boiler showing smoke box and uptake in place. This is a much later sketch of an improved type of Scotch boiler. The *Titanic*'s boilers worked under natural draught conditions using no forced draught fans or preheater air tubes. *(Authors' Collections)*

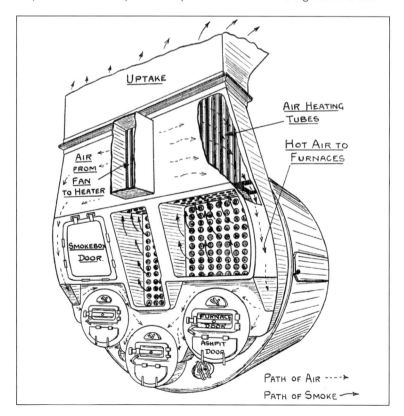

interval for firing was set by the Engineer of the Watch at the Starting Platform.

In each boiler room a gong on the indicator would sound at the required interval and display the number of the furnace to be fired.

By having five indicators in each stokehold and one for each boiler, the timing could be staggered so that the minimum number of furnace doors would be open at the same time, and no opposite doors on double-ended boilers open together. So it was that in the early 1920s, when coal burning gave way to oil-fired boilers and Kilroy's apparatus was made redundant, firemen may have joked about the conditions of the coal burners with comments like 'Kilroy was here'.

Firemen's and trimmers' duties

At the bottom of the Engine Room structure were the trimmers who worked in the hot airless bunkers where the gloomy atmosphere was thick with stifling coal dust. Here they filled barrows with coal from the bunkers which was then tipped on the steel plate decking beneath the furnace mouths.

The trimmer upended his barrow next to the fireman who tended the furnaces. Under each double-ended boiler there were three furnaces at each end, each with a separate door. To conserve heat doors were never opened at the same time.

The task of the firemen of keeping the furnaces at full blast demanded a good standard of physical fitness, strength and stamina. The first job was to clean out one of the furnaces which had already been prepared by a process known as 'burning down'. The fire bars were then cleared of 'clinkers', or white hot masses of fused slag and impurities, which caused an obstruction to air for combustion, and had to be removed by dousing with water and breaking up. They were dislodged by a slice bar, known as a 'tommy' or 'jumbo', an extra-long poker over 40lb in weight, for reaching the rear of the furnace. The tommy was thrust home four times, once along each track of the grate, which showered ashes down

RIGHT White Star historian John Siggins with a 9ft ash shovel from the *Olympic*. The ash shovel was used for removing lighter ashes and clinker from the ashpit under the grate of the furnace. These would then be shovelled into wheelbarrows and disposed of in the ash ejectors. The shovel was long enough to reach the full length of the ashpit. *(John Siggins)*

into the ashpit and raised the clinkers to the top of the coals.

The next operation was to rake out the clinkers in their white-hot state on to the plates using a 9ft-long steel implement like a large garden hoe. These were quenched by hosing down with water. The trimmers then shovelled out the fragments and raked out ashes that littered the deck into barrows and emptied them into the See's Ash Ejector, a receptacle connected to the side of the ship by a pipe through which water pressure forced or blew the waste material into the sea. This was known as 'shooting the ashes'.

While the trimmers were disposing of the ashes, a fireman would be feeding a small amount of slack to the burned-down furnace. This was known as 'coaling the bars', after which it was worked up to full capacity. In the meantime, plenty of coal had been heaped on to the plates, and the firemen would begin stoking up, making sure to adjust the draught lever before opening the furnace door. Failure to do this could result in a 'blowback', a searing hot flame shooting out across the stokehold. A 'pitch' of coal (about a dozen shovelsful or around 132lb of coal) was then thrown on each

fire and the door slammed tight. This stoking-up required a certain degree of precision, as the furnace door aperture was only just wider than the shovel or 'banjo'. After the fire had burned for a while, a two-pronged rake (sometimes referred to as a 'devil') was used for levelling off the spread of coal to an effective depth of 4in along the length of the grate. When boilers were at full blast, maximum steam pressure was indicated on the brass pressure gauge above the fires with its needle pointing to the red zone on the gauge scale. This was called 'keeping her in the blood'. In addition, a watchful eye was kept on the water gauge glass to ensure there was sufficient water in the boiler.

In rough weather, firemen learned to stoke as the ship's bow plunged down, slamming the door shut as the ship rose again, to avoid a shower of red-hot coals on their feet.

Ash ejection

When fires had to be sliced or raked, the remnants of clinkers and ashes dropped into the ashpit below the grate from where air fanned the furnaces. Large ships like the *Titanic* consumed some 850 tons of coal each day which resulted, after burning, in around 100 tons of ash that had to be disposed of with the ship underway at sea. There were two See's Ash Ejectors in each of the large boiler rooms, Nos 2–6, recessed into the coal bunkers.

To use the ash ejector:
(i) Open the lid on the hopper (W) and see that it and the discharge pipe are clear of water and ashes.
(ii) Open valve (Z) on ship's side by pulling down on lever linkage handle and start duplex feed pump in adjoining room and wait until gauge (M) reaches a pressure of 150psi.
(iii) Open cock (P) near stokehold floor and continuously shovel ashes into the hopper.
The velocity of water in the pipe and hopper entrained the ashes as they were dumped into the hopper and they were carried up the discharge pipe and overboard.

When the *Titanic* and *Olympic* were alongside or in port approaches, four Railton, Campbell & Crawford's steam-assisted ash hoists were used instead and the ashes transferred to barges alongside.

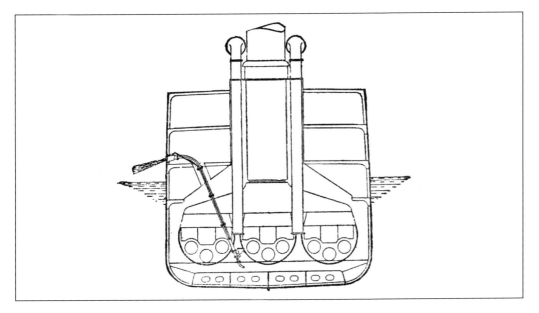

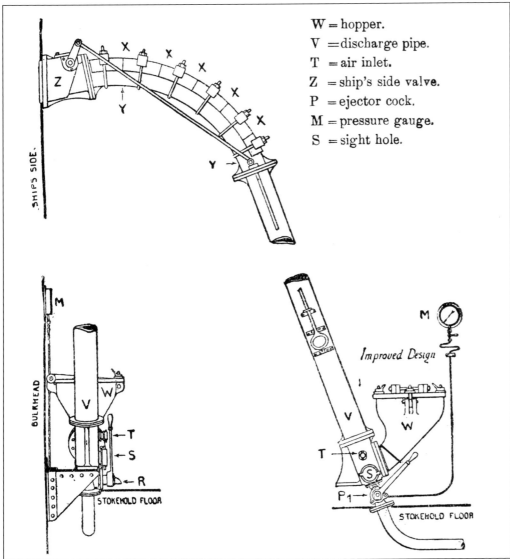

W = hopper.
V = discharge pipe.
T = air inlet.
Z = ship's side valve.
P = ejector cock.
M = pressure gauge.
S = sight hole.

Improved Design

Coal

Coal was normally brought alongside the ship in port by coal barges. Before loading into the bunkers every ventilator cowl was covered with canvas, any air vent louvres were closed and all interior spaces sealed off and where possible access doors and companionways kept shut. The coal was transferred in large quarter-ton buckets into the coaling ports. These ports were openings in the shell plating, some 10ft

above the waterline, with bottom-hinged flaps that could take a temporary sheet-iron scoop. In addition, a row of simple derricks could be rigged above, the heels of which located into concave indentations in the hull, together with precarious two-man platforms adjacent to each coaling port. The coal buckets were winched up from the barge and tipped into the port, and the coal then cascaded down a chute into the bunker. Generally two ports served each bunker. It could take up to 24 hours to coal a large liner like the *Titanic*.

Before coaling, the ship's carpenter went over the ship's side to remove the eight bolts that secured each coaling port shut. Following bunkering, the carpenter sealed up the ports with a buckram gasket that had been soaked in red lead, for water tightness. In addition, every railing, deck, companionway and passageway had to be cleaned thoroughly.

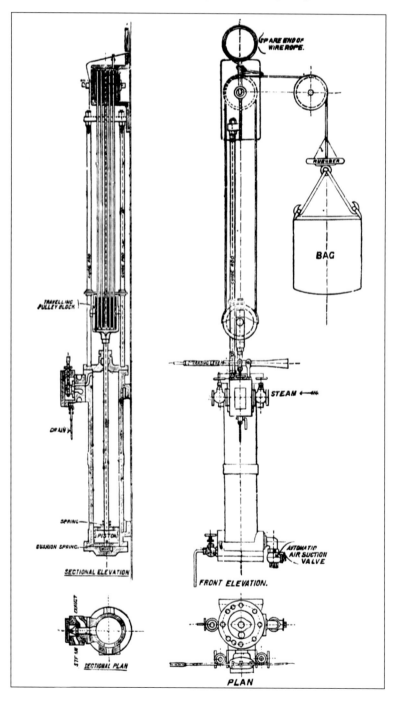

BELOW **The manually operated ash hoist was used mainly when the ship was alongside in port.** *(The Shipbuilder)*

Calorific values of solid fuels

Heating (calorific) values in British Thermal Units per pound (Btu/lb) of some of the solid fuels used in the liners of the day:

Fuel	Heating value (Btu/lb of fuel)
Best Welsh coal	16,000
Average Newcastle coal	14,900
Average Derbyshire coal	13,900
Average Lancashire coal	13,900
Average Scotch coal	14,200

Newcastle and Scotch coal burned much faster than Welsh, but did not give out such an intense local heat. With Welsh coal there was little or no flame, and very little smoke.

Inspection, common defects and repairs to Scotch boilers

A range of defects could be encountered in boilers with some years' service behind them. Any running repairs could be carried out by the engineers on board after first shutting down the boiler in question and taking it out of service. Dockside and dry-dock repairs would be carried out by skilled boilermakers during routine maintenance when the boiler was shut down and drained. There could be anything up to 28 items on a schedule for inspection

Danger of fire in bunkers

When coal was stored in the bunkers, especially when they were adjacent to the boilers, the possibility of spontaneous combustion was always present.

Coal, when exposed to the air, rapidly absorbs oxygen and this oxidation produces heat. If the coal has been freshly worked, it gives off a gas known as 'marsh gas' (methane), which is combustible when the atmosphere contains certain percentages of gas, such as 5½% or 20%. If the atmosphere contains 10% of marsh gas, the mixture is highly explosive. Heat is produced when a chemical action takes place and if the temperature reaches 1,200°F (the ignition point of marsh gas), then fire breaks out in the coal and generally this occurred in the centre of the coal in the bunker space.

The gas is lighter than air, so surface ventilation is necessary to carry it away and whenever possible bunker lids or hatches were removed in fine weather to facilitate this. As far as was possible the bunkers were worked out in the order in which the coal was supplied. In this way coal was prevented from remaining in the bunkers for an indefinite period.

The presence of marsh gas (methane) was detected by means of a safety lamp, which when turned low burned with a blue cap when the gas was present. It is not known whether such devices were in use on the *Titanic*.

Small bunker fires, if caught in time, were extinguished by means of sand, which smothered the flame, but more serious, deeply seated fires had to be dug out if it was practicable and the burning coals removed completely. When water or steam was used to extinguish a bunker fire, large volumes had to be used, otherwise 'water gas' was generated which in turn exacerbated an already dangerous situation. If it was at all possible, the bunker space was sealed off completely to starve the fire of oxygen from the air.

The *Titanic* would normally have been bunkered with best Welsh coal, but as at the time she entered service there was a national coal strike, she was bunkered with a mix of various coals in addition to best Welsh, as a smouldering fire in No. 10 bunker on the starboard side of boiler room No. 6 ignited when she left Belfast.

and repair in one single-ended Scotch boiler – for the *Titanic* this routine would have to be repeated another 52 times.

Scaling and cleaning

The enemies of efficient heat transfer were soot, a product of combustion on the inside of the fire tubes, and scale on their water side. In addition, scale on the inside of the plates and any oil in the water could form deposits on the surface and cause 'hot spots'.

When the boiler was cold, it was usually entered via the manholes. All steam and water valves were first screwed down shut by their spindles. Scale was then removed from the furnace and combustion chamber plates by chipping and scraping, with care being taken not to damage the fire tubes. Any traces of oil on the shell plates, near the working water level, were carefully removed. Oil deposited on plate surfaces during the blowing-down process was removed and the plates washed with soda and water. Finally, after scaling, the boiler water spaces were thoroughly washed down with a hose and all scale and dirt was removed by being raked out through the bottom manhole doors.

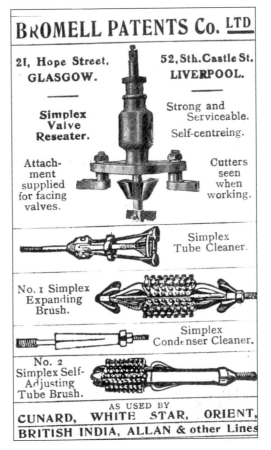

LEFT Advertisement for boiler cleaning implements.
(The Shipbuilder)

Sweeping the tubes

The smoke or fire tubes were swept out by spiral wound wire brushes screwed on to a long rod, which was pushed through each straight tube. The action was carried out during maintenance periods with the smokebox doors removed. The cleaning of double-ended boilers was from the boiler front through to the combustion chamber. The soot and ashes were then removed from the furnace and combustion chamber and all burnt or broken firebars renewed.

Repair of a leaking boiler tube

Boiler tubes generally leaked at their back ends. They were repaired by re-expanding, or by driving a tapered ferrule into the tube similar to that done with locomotive boiler tubes. Alternatively, the tube ends could be cut off flush with the back tube plate, and then driven through from the front end, following which they would be expanded. However, this was not considered good practice on ageing tubes.

Repair of a split boiler tube at sea

In the case of a boiler tube splitting at sea it was necessary to be stopped entirely, but first the boiler fires had to be drawn down from the furnace belonging to the box of tubes in which the leaky tube was situated. A mild steel rod of the requisite length and of about 1in or so diameter was threaded for 2–3in at each end and then inserted though the split tube. Two large washers were then turned with a rebate that entered each end of the tube with the larger diameter flush with the tube ends and with nuts on the threads. These were then tightened up to secure the washers and prevent water entering the boiler.

Changing a gauge glass

The boiler gauge glasses would in time become discoloured by scale or dirt and were replaced by new ones held as spares. The procedure was the same as for changing a broken gauge glass, which required more urgent attention.

1. First the water and steam cocks were shut and the drain cock opened and the three-sided ½in heavy glass guard was removed to gain access to the glass.
2. The gland nuts on the glass were slackened.
3. A blank nut in the top casting of the gauge was removed and the glass was then taken vertically through the access hole in the housing.
4. The gland nuts were then carefully cleaned and checked to ensure that they ran freely on their threads. New sealing packing in the form of tapered 'woodite' rings was fitted on to a new gauge glass. The new gauge glass was slid in through the top access hole and located in the bottom water end as far as it would go. The gland nuts were hand-tightened as much as possible, the blank nut re-located and the guard replaced.
5. With the drain cock still open, the steam cock was opened until steam blew through the glass to the drain cock. In this way the new glass would be heated up before the full boiler pressure was applied to it. The water cock was then opened slowly and the drain cock closed. At this stage full pressure was on the gauge glass, with the water indicating the correct water level, and the water gauge completely tested. Steam and water cocks were always opened slowly.

The surviving No. 25 gauge glass from the *Olympic*. (John Siggins)

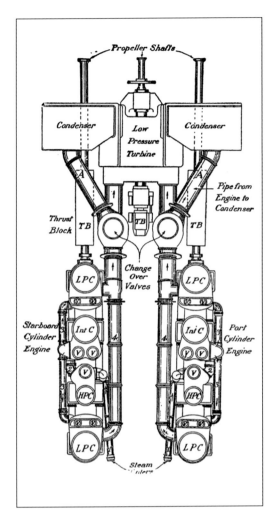

Steam reciprocating engines: the facts

Diameter (bore) of cylinders	54in, 84in, 97in, 97in
Stroke	75in
Type of valves fitted	Piston valves on HP and IP cylinders
Type of valve gear	Stephenson link motion
Type of piston rings fitted	Lockwood & Carlisle on all cylinder pistons, except HP, and on all piston valves. The HP rings were of the Ramsbottom type.
Diameter of HP and IP piston rods (high tensile steel)	14in
Diameter of LP piston rods	11¾in
Diameter of HP and IP connecting rods	13½in–15in
Diameter of LP connecting rods	11½in–13in
Diameter and length of top ends (HP and LP)	16½in x 17¼in
Diameter and length of top ends (LP)	13½in x 14¼in
Diameter of crank pins	27¾in with 9in hole
Length of crank pins (HP and IP)	35in
Length of crank pins (LP)	24in
Diameter of crankshaft	27in with 9in hole
Speed/max speed	75/85 rpm

LEFT Plan view of the triple expansion engines and exhaust turbine, driving three screws. This layout on the Olympic Class had originally been trialled in White Star's *Laurentic* of 1909. *(Authors' Collections)*

BELOW The *Titanic*'s starboard (left) and port (right) main engines under construction. In the bottom right-hand corner may be seen the piston valves, 'D' slide valves and cylinder covers ready for assembly. *(UFTM H1710)*

Main propulsion machinery

Steam reciprocating engines

The *Titanic*'s combination machinery was arranged as the plan of the triple expansion engine layout shown above.

For each cylinder, steam from the boilers was admitted to the high-pressure cylinder, and then the exhaust steam from these was led via steam slide valve gear to the intermediate or medium-pressure cylinder (Int. C), and from here the steam was exhausted via steam slide valve into two low-pressure cylinders at either end of the engine.

As the pressure decreased the volume of the steam increased, hence the increase in cylinder bore diameters from 54in, 84in and 97in and accordingly the increase in cylinder volume.

Typical state of the steam at these stages was as follows:

HP inlet 215psi	394°F
IP inlet 78psi	322°F
LP inlet 24psi	266°F
Turbine inlet 9psi (abs)	188°F
Turbine outlet 1psi (abs)	102°F

From the two LP cylinders, steam at sub-atmospheric pressure passed to the Parsons exhaust turbine (the low-pressure turbine) on the central propeller shaft, where steam further passed through it before finally exhausting into the condenser to be turned back into water for recirculation via extraction pumps and feed pumps back to the boilers.

From the plan on page 91 it may be seen that the steam from the main triple expansion engines could either be led to the turbine or it could be directed straight to the condensers via large 'changeover' valves, thus effectively 'short-

RIGHT End view of port main engine under construction. This view shows the low-pressure cylinder and beneath is the toothed flywheel with steam-assisted turning gear disengaged. In the foreground are what appear to be two eccentric sheaves before fitting. The Harland & Wolff employee to the right of the picture gives some idea of the massive size of the engine. *(UFTM H1711)*

circuiting' the LP turbine. This latter operation would normally be done upon entering or leaving port or under similar conditions in confined waters where the *Titanic* had to be manoeuvred like a twin-screw vessel. The exhaust turbine would be engaged when she was 'Full Away' on passage in the open sea.

According to an engineer who served on board the 1927-built *Laurentic*, installed with a later type but not a radical development of the *Titanic*'s combination machinery, the central shaft, when engaged, 'had no effect on the speed' but 'it took the knocks out of the engines'.

BELOW **Installation of the engines in the Engine Room of the *Britannic*. This shows one end of a crankshaft in place on the engine bed. The main bearings have been fitted into place and the open flat plates show where the main engine support columns will be fitted.** *(UFTM H1996)*

RIGHT Profile and plan
views of the four-crank
triple expansion engine.
The large, low-pressure
cylinders are at both
ends. In between the
support columns on
the profile drawing may
be seen the ahead and
astern connecting rods
that were driven by
eccentrics on the main
crankshaft.
(Authors' Collections)

BELOW This diagram
shows a low-pressure
piston without its
integral slide valve
case and mechanism.
As in the *Titanic*,
it shows the main
crosshead illustrated
between two guide
shoes. The piston
crown is very slightly
conical, almost flat, as
would have been the
case on the *Titanic*.
(Authors' Collections)

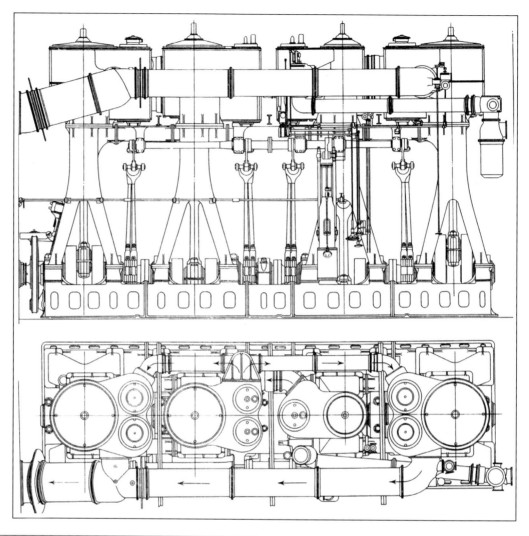

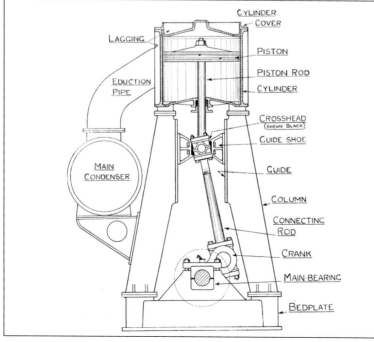

Titanic's main engines were balanced on
the Yarrow, Schlick & Tweedy system whereby
vibration of the main crankshafts during
rotation was minimised by the crank angles
and sequence being staggered. Considering
the port engine, looking forward with anti-
clockwise rotation, starting with the HP
piston at top dead centre (TDC), the following
sequence took place: HP at TDC then 106°
for the IP piston to be at TDC, then 100° for
the forward LP cylinder to be at TDC followed
by a further 54° for the after LP to arrive at
TDC, and finally 100° to bring the HP piston
back to TDC.

To get some idea of the terms and major
components used in reciprocating machinery
a generic section through a low-pressure
cylinder of a steam reciprocating steam engine
is shown on the left.

Major machinery failures that required

repairs to be carried out by Harland & Wolff shoreside engineers when in the UK or the ship's engineers when in the United States were: a broken connecting rod, cracked main piston, broken piston rings, cracked/sheared crankshaft, main bearing wiped, crosshead bearings wiped, leaking glands.

Mechanism of a slide valve

The *Titanic*'s main engines were double-acting, whereby steam would expand and push the piston down towards the crankshaft and then steam would be admitted to the underside of the piston to drive it back up. To enable this to happen, and change over the steam distribution, a mechanism known as a slide valve was used which was timed, controlled and driven from the main crankshaft by an eccentric strap (eccentric in that the slide/ piston valves drive crank was offset from the centre of the main engine crankshaft). On the *Titanic*'s main engines, the HP cylinder was provided with a single piston valve and the IP cylinder with two piston valves, similarly operated to the twin slide valves on the LP cylinders. In these cases the twin valve push rods were joined to a common yoke driven by a central connecting rod from the Stephenson's Link Motion; the reversing gear for each set was operated by a Brown engine such that the valves could be repositioned when it was desired to manoeuvre astern.

The slide valves used on the *Titanic*'s HP and IP cylinders were of the piston valve type. As its name implies, the piston has the form of a piston with two glands. As the steam pressure acted all round the valve it was self-balancing.

Stuffing boxes and glands

On main engine piston rods and slide valve rods and with all other steam-driven auxiliary machinery it was necessary to 'seal' the steam into the piston area to prevent steam and condensate leakage. The main reason for this was to enable the steam to expand and use its energy effectively and also to protect the oil in the sump of the main engines from contamination by water.

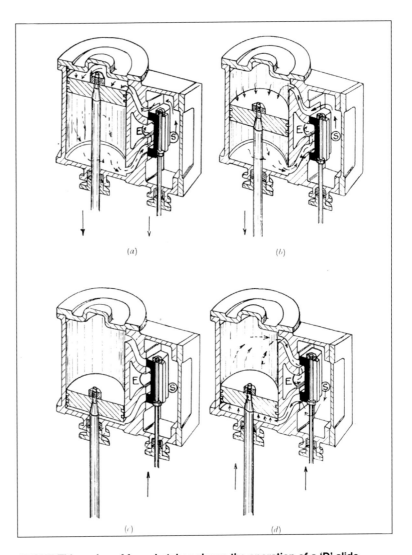

ABOVE This series of four sketches shows the operation of a 'D' slide valve. Only the *Titanic*'s four low-pressure cylinders were fitted with 'D' slide valves; the intermediate and high-pressures were fitted with piston valves. *(Authors' Collections)*

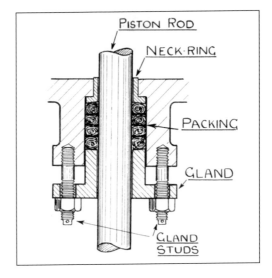

LEFT A generic sketch of a stuffing box and gland for a piston rod. Its main function was to maintain steam tightness, but at the same time to allow a rod or shaft to move with minimum friction and wear. This was always a difficult balance to achieve. *(Authors' Collections)*

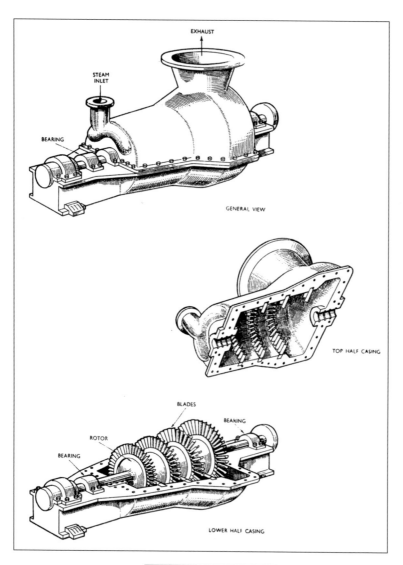

STEAM INLET

EXHAUST

BEARING

GENERAL VIEW

TOP HALF CASING

BLADES

BEARING

ROTOR

BEARING

LOWER HALF CASING

ABOVE Unlike the reciprocating engine which has many moving parts, the turbine consists of only two main parts – the casing, which is fixed, and the rotor, which is carried in two bearings only and revolves inside the casing by the action of the steam.
(Authors' Collections)

Low-pressure turbine: the facts

Turbine type	Parsons direct-coupled, low-pressure reaction
Turbine mass	420 tons
Rotor and blades mass	130 tons
Diameter of rotor drum	12ft
Length of rotor drum	13ft 8in
Length overall of turbine	49ft
Number of blade expansions	6*
Blade height (1st expansion)	18 in
Blade height (2nd expansion)	21½in*
Blade height (3rd expansion)	25½in
Blade height (4th expansion)	25½in
Blade height (5th expansion)	25½in
Blade height (6th expansion)	25½in
No of blade rows on rotor	42
Speed/ max speed	165/190rpm

*Figures for *Britannic's* LP turbine

Low-pressure exhaust turbine

The turbine was built to the Parsons multi-stage reaction design with blade lengths ranging from 18–25½in in order that the expanded steam from the main reciprocating engines should expend further energy through the turbine before finally exhausting to the condenser. At full speed exhaust steam from the two main reciprocating engines entered the turbine at 9psi absolute (or –5.7psi gauge) and further expanded through the turbine blades until it exited the turbine at 1psi absolute (or –13.7psi gauge).

The turbine directly drove the *Titanic's* centre four-bladed, cast manganese bronze propeller. The turbine exhaust outlets evenly split and passed into the tops of the two condensers located outboard and abeam of the turbine, via large-diameter ducting. Mounted between the turbine outlets and the inlets to the condensers were two huge swiss sluice valves that operated in a similar fashion to watertight doors. An electric motor operated these and the gate of the sluice valve was moved horizontally, thus completely sealing off the turbine from operation when not required.

Under normal manoeuvring conditions in and out of port or at 'Slow Ahead' and steaming astern, the *Titanic's* outer screws were used and the centre screw driven by the LP turbine was by-passed so that the ship manoeuvred and steered like a conventional twin-screw vessel. When required, two huge changeover valves of the piston type were activated by a Brown's steam engine which operated a link mechanism. The changeover valves' pistons covered or uncovered a series of circumferential ports to the LP turbine or directly to the condenser. In the upper position the ports were open to the turbine and in the lower position the steam was admitted to the condenser. Both valve pistons were operated by a rocker arm connected to the crosshead of a Brown's steam and hydraulic engine, which actuated both valves simultaneously. The Brown's engine was controlled by a lever on the Starting Platform close to the main reversing gear.

When the ship's engines were sufficiently

LEFT The *Britannic*'s rotor suspended above the turbine lower casing in the Turbine Shop. The positioning of the turbine in its lower casing and the fitting of the top half of the casing was extremely critical. Rotor and casing were guided into place by location columns to ensure blading and labyrinth fins did not foul and that the rotor would rest aligned in its bearings. *(UFTM H2155)*

BELOW The *Britannic*'s low-pressure turbine with its centre shaft ready for coupling clearly visible. *(UFTM H2165)*

BELOW The low-pressure turbine secured in its position in the *Britannic*'s Turbine Engine Room. The location where the large swiss sluice valves were to be fitted can be seen to the top left where a working party of men are standing. *(UFTM H2164)*

Maintenance and repairs on the *Olympic*'s low-pressure exhaust turbine

The LP exhaust turbine was an intrinsically sealed engine, balanced prior to installation. Once running, one of the few things that still needed to be maintained were the main bearings at its forward and after ends, ensuring they were kept topped up to the correct level with lubrication oil. In port or during the time it was stationary but ready for use, the turbine was 'warmed through' with auxiliary steam.

The main thing that could go wrong with the turbine was that the moving blades on the rotor could foul the fixed blades in the casing, thereby stripping up to a whole row of blades. Blades could fail through what we now know to be 'root fatigue' (they vibrated like a tuning fork when in motion). A way of overcoming this was to strengthen the blades circumferentially by means of stiff brass wire near the blade tips, which was in turn bound with copper wire and all soldered together, thus reducing the vibrational effect.

The only problem with the stiffening of blades was that their constant expansion and contraction could lead to the stiffening and binding wire breaking (due to fatigue) in addition to any galvanic corrosion caused between the blade and wire materials.

High temperatures and centrifugal motion, which could also cause irregular blade extension due to expansion, resulted in the blades fouling the casing. In such cases blade replacement to the rotor and casing could only be carried out by the builders, which meant that the turbine casing would have to be split open and the rotor raised and removed to the blading workshop ashore.

Some periodic maintenance reports gained from operational experience on the *Olympic*'s LP turbine have been recorded and are reproduced here verbatim.

As early as October 1911 Harland & Wolff had written to the Board of Trade about its concern that the BoT wanted to inspect the turbine: 'We had hoped that you would have considered the inspection of the steam and exhaust ends and the inside of the rotor drum, sufficient, but we will arrange for lifting the [turbine] cover as desired.'

On account of the cooperation and goodwill by the builders, White Star was initially given permission by the Board of Trade in a letter dated 27 March 1912:

> to lift the turbine casing cover triennially instead of annually, provided no defects were observed or suspected. The principal reason for the concession being that the turbine is fitted to obtain some additional energy from steam previously used in the reciprocating engines, which would otherwise be left; and that the vessel would still be a first class high-speed ship when working with reciprocating engines only.

However, during *Olympic*'s 1912–13 refit, the turbine was opened up and repair and maintenance of an unspecified nature was completed. In early April 1913 the BoT decided to keep a particularly close eye on *Olympic*'s low-pressure turbine, for during her early years of service it became apparent that it was prone to excessive wear.

Notwithstanding the repairs carried out in

BELOW A sectional drawing of a typical low-pressure turbine showing the wiring of the blades.
(Authors' Collections)

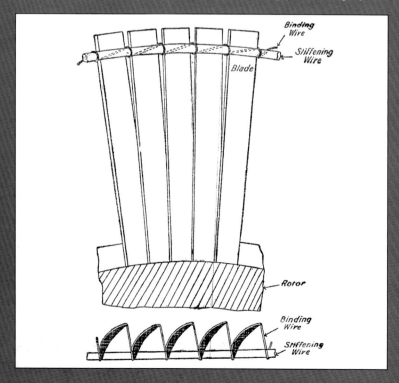

March 1913, when *Olympic*'s annual survey was due early in 1914 the turbine casing was lifted again. The surveyors felt it was necessary to lift the rotor as well, and 'as a result of careful inspection some 500 fractures of the binding wires were discovered':

> These fractures were spread throughout the turbine, in the top and bottom casing and in the rotor, being for the most part in the two rings of binding wire nearest the ends of the blades; and being more numerous at the steam end of the turbine although not confined to that end.
>
> In some cases, adjacent fractures had practically isolated small groups of blades from radial support.
>
> Two blades were found to be broken, one in the casing and one on the rotor. In one case the broken part, about 5in in length, had lodged longitudinally between two adjacent blades in such a position that if displaced by shock or vibration serious damage to the blading would have followed.
>
> In the other case the blade had probably been broken prior to the last survey as the loose part was not found.

As the White Star Line gained further operational experience with the turbine, they made the decision to repair it by modifying the original design of the blade tips:

> On account of their recent experience of the unequal expansions which may take place when warming up a turbine of this size, the owners decided at this survey to increase the end clearance of the blades.
>
> The blade ends throughout the turbine were accordingly filed down to gauge, to allow of approximately $\frac{1}{8}$in instead of $\frac{1}{10}$in.

This procedure would have been carried out with the rotor mounted on a very large lathe and rotated so that each blade was ground by a fixed end grinder in order to gain repeatability and consistency of clearance.

It is interesting to note the conditions observed in service, as the *Olympic* settled into a regular routine. Of the turbine's 1914 survey a source which is assumed to be the surveyor reported:

The central propeller of the *Olympic* is now used more freely when manoeuvring than was the practice when the vessel first came out, it having been found that her steering qualities are thus much improved.

> The reciprocating engines must be running at about half speed before the turbine can be started from rest; and at sea the revolutions require to be more than 25 per minute to maintain it in action when exhaust steam is solely relied upon.
>
> An auxiliary steam connection was provided at Belfast last year [1913] by means of which steam reduced to 25psi is supplied through an 8½in diam. pipe connected with both of the main steam pipes to the turbine, which are 61in in diameter.
>
> It has been suggested that this arrangement is responsible for the trouble with binding wires, but as the initial pressure of the auxiliary steam is only 25psi, the difference in area of the auxiliary and main steam supply pipes is so great, and as according to the statement of the Chief Engineer, no appreciable rise in pressure is indicated by the turbine steam gauge when the auxiliary steam valve is opened, I am of the opinion that the use of the connection in question is not the cause of the failure of the wires.
>
> It has also been suggested that unequal expansion in the huge castings forming the turbine casing and in the rotor, when in the process of warming before use, has caused sections of blades to beat heavily at the ends, forcing the binding wires out of alignment and causing ultimate fracture. This view probably led to the decision to increase the end clearance.
>
> Having carefully considered the circumstances in the case of this turbine, and the position and appearance of the fractures, I am of the opinion that the principal cause of failure of binding wires is the overheating to which the wires are subjected when being brazed.

The turbine seems to have proved satisfactory for the rest of the *Olympic*'s career, although some damaged blading required removal in September 1933.

up to speed at 'Half Ahead' (about 50 rev/min or around 13.5kt), the Brown's engine was operated to activate the valves from by-pass to engage the turbine, which gave the _Titanic_ an extra 2kt at 'Half Ahead', bringing her up to 15.5kt. The turbine speed could be increased proportionally by the amount of steam received from the main engines, up to a maximum of 190 rev/min at full speed.

The changeover valves were capable of a form of speed regulation as there was an automatic override whereby the turbine's speed activated a Proell centrifugal governor. This in turn actuated the Brown's engine, which operated the changeover valves. If the speed of the turbine rotor exceeded 10% above the maximum of the number of revolutions set, then the changeover valves would redirect the steam directly to the condensers until the speed of the turbine dropped below the preset desired revolutions.

One of the inherent problems of the LP turbine was its steam tightness. It was not so much that of steam leaking out, but because of its sub-atmospheric or partial-vacuum condition, it was that of air trying to enter the turbine. In part this was achieved by the seal formed by the butting flange surfaces on the upper and lower casings of the turbine. These were machine-ground flat and then finished off by 'hand scraping', a laborious task that could take a week. There was no gasket or sealant used for the mating faces,

but sometimes a thin film of 'triple-boiled oil' was applied and the casing nuts and studs tightened down. The turbine shafts were 'sealed' at either end of the casing by 'labyrinth' glands which minimised the ingress of air into the turbine. At each end of the casing this consisted of ten circumferential fins on the turbine rotor with ten fins let into the casing. These fins had a radial clearance of about 0.010in ('10 thou'). Outside these fins were four Ramsbottom-type piston-type rings set into the shaft. The gland was thereby divided into 19 or so annular spaces, which were connected via a pipe and valve to an auxiliary low-pressure steam supply. Sufficient steam was then admitted to produce atmospheric pressure and the existence of this pressure prevented the ingress of air. Often a slight weep of steam into the atmosphere would be observed.

Condensers

Function

The surface condenser was so-called because condensation of the steam took place on the surface of a large number of tubes through which cold sea water was circulated. The condenser was the heat exchanger in which the steam was condensed back to water after doing work in the engines.

The main functions of the condenser were:

1. To reduce the back pressure on the main reciprocating units and LP turbine and so enable the engines to develop greater power.
2. To enable the steam to be expanded in the main engines' LP cylinders and the LP turbine to a lower pressure than would be possible if the steam was exhausted to the atmosphere.
3. To enable the working substance (water) to be used over and over again.

Condensers: the facts	
No of condensers	2
Length	20ft
Height	24ft
Diameter and material of tubes	7/8in; 60/40 brass (Muntz metal)
Number tubes/condenser	9,500 approx
Cooling surface/condenser	25,275ft²

LEFT Condensers
leaving the works.
(UFTM H1980)

BELOW One of
the *Olympic*'s main
condensers with its
casing partly removed
in the Engine Works.
(UFTM H1458)

After passing through the LP turbine the steam had expanded down to 1psi absolute (or −13.7psi gauge or 28½in of vacuum, *i.e.* sub-atmospheric) in the two condensers. The exhausted steam was condensed by coming into contact with the outer surface of the nest of tubes through which sea water was pumped by the sea-water circulating pump. A Weir's air pump was also needed to extract the air and condensed water from the bottom of the condenser. Air came into the condenser from the steam, but, unlike the steam, it could not be condensed and was therefore removed to maintain a high vacuum in the condenser.

The exhausted steam exited the turbine casing through two large rectangular openings on either side leading to each condenser. As previously mentioned, the steam could also be led directly to the condensers, by-passing the LP turbine, when the main reciprocating engines were running astern or at less than half speed. When the exhausted steam entered the condenser from the top it was directed downwards, impinging on the manifold of tubes in the main chamber. Simultaneously, cold sea water was circulated through the tubes and heat was removed from the steam and exchanged to the cold tubes causing the water vapour to condense on the tubes in droplets. These would then fall under gravity to the bottom of the condenser chamber. The fresh water collected was then pumped through the return feed system back to the boilers.

Construction

Harland & Wolff's design of condensers were
pear-shaped (sometimes known as heart-
shaped) in section, and the inlet to these ran
the full length of the condenser. The pear-
shaped construction was designed such that
the steam entering was caused to traverse the
cooling surfaces at practically uniform velocity
throughout its passage.

There were no baffle plates or partitions in
the body of the condenser so the incoming
steam entered and distributed itself over the
whole length and breadth of the condenser. As
it cooled it shrank in volume and dropped to the
bottom of the divergent area of the condenser
chamber which accommodated the smaller
volume of the condensate. The construction of
the pear-shaped condenser was of a cast-iron
chamber flanged at each end to accommodate
1in-thick rolled brass tube plates at each end.
These plates were drilled with holes $7/8$in in
diameter through which passed some 9,500
Muntz metal tubes per condenser, with a
supporting plate in the centre. For each tube
at both ends small stuffing boxes or ferrules
were fitted to prevent the leakage of sea water
between plate and tube.

As sea water proved ideal for the condenser
cooling, water was drawn from inlets on the
underside of the *Titanic*'s hull near the turn of
the bilge, circulated through the condensers via
two high-volume sea-water circulating pumps
and discharged through two outlets just above
the waterline. The *Titanic*'s two condensers had
a combined cooling surface area of 50,550ft².
Her auxiliary condenser for ancillary machinery,
and which was also used in port, was sited on
the starboard side of the main engine room; it
had a cooling surface of 3,600ft².

Maintenance

Although the condensers contained no
moving parts, it was necessary to overhaul
them regularly to maintain their efficiency. The
outside (steam side) of the tubes could become
coated with a film of oil or grease carried
over by steam from the engines. The usual
operational procedure to clean this side was to
fill the steam side up with fresh water to which
was added a good strong solution of soda.
Steam would then be piped to the bottom of
the condenser and the solution left to boil for
several hours, after which it was discharged to
the bilges.

On the sea-water side, the inside of the
tubes would in time foul up with a scaly deposit
or become choked with mud, grit or small shells
depending on the waters in which the ship had

been steaming. Cleaning was generally carried out during dry-docking because of the work involved in removing the large condenser doors. The blocked tubes would be rodded out with a large wire spiral brush or tube-scraper, similar to the way in which the Scotch boiler fire tubes were cleaned.

Leaking or split condenser tubes were usually detected by a rise in the water level or increased density of the boiler water. If it was not convenient to fit new tubes, the defective ones were blanked off by driving in wooden plugs at either end of the offending tube. Later, blank-ended ferrules were used to replace the open-ended ones.

Feed-water filters

The condensate from the condensers was drawn off by extraction or air pumps and delivered to two 2,790gal feed tanks from which it drained into two 48ft³ hotwell tanks. It was in these tanks that any fresh water was made up from the ship's three evaporators to compensate for any leakage in the steam cycle system. From the hotwells, the feed water was extracted by two pairs of Weir's hotwell pumps. One pair served each tank and discharged to two pairs of feed-water filters. The feed-water filters were placed in the feed system to remove any suspended impurities (mainly oil) from the

feed water. In a reciprocating engine the pistons and slide valves required constant lubrication. Some of the oil would become entrained in the steam and, unless removed, would be pumped back into the boiler. This would result in some of the heating surfaces becoming coated and as a result would cause overheating with a consequent loss of strength.

In the *Titanic*, the filters were situated between the condensate extraction (air) pumps and the boiler feed pumps whereby the water flowed through the filters due to the force of gravity. There were four placed against the forward engine room bulkhead. They were supplied by Railton, Campbell & Crawford and had a total filtering area of 1,008ft².

Operation and cleaning of feed-water filters

Inside the filter vessel was an element made up of 26 perforated plates (like a giant version of a cafetiere plunger), in between which were placed disc-shaped sheets of felt or 'Terry' towelling to form a super sandwich. On the filter vessel inlet and outlet valves, a by-pass valve and a pressure differential valve were fitted. Also fitted was a soda cock with steam inlet and at the bottom of the filter vessel was a drain cock. The assembled filter element would be horizontally located on a spindle and secured

LEFT The *Titanic*'s main feed filters with their covers and filter elements removed prior to installation in the Engine Room. *(The Shipbuilder)*

with a nut inside the chamber. A cast-iron cover secured with 24 nuts completed the unit.

As the filter element clogged with oil or particles collected as the feed water passed through the filter, the differential gauge indicated the degree of silt and clogging that occurred. At some predetermined pressure indication, say about 15psi, the filter was isolated by opening the by-pass valve and shutting the inlet and outlet valves. The soda cock, having been filled with soda, was then opened while the filter was full of water and steam was allowed to boil the element and towelling cloth. Any impurities in the intercepting material would be freed to fall to the bottom of the vessel. The drain cock was opened to allow any silt or sludge and the water to drain out. Any resulting drain cock blockage had to be cleared. Following this the whole filter assembly was blown through with steam before putting the filter back on stream.

When the filter differential pressure rose to about 25psi above the usual pressure, the towelling cloth or felt was cleaned or changed.

Thrust collars and blocks

The action of a ship powering through the water is affected by the reaction of the screw(s) against a horizontal column of water, which is pushed astern away from the vessel. This resulted in an equal push forward against the propeller shaft, amounting in large ships to some hundreds of tons. If this thrust were not harnessed in some way it would try to push the engine crankshaft and the connecting rods and piston rods would be forced out of line and strained by the forward movement caused by the thrust of the propeller. The thrust block and its collars were installed to prevent this tendency and were the arrangement whereby the thrust of a propeller was applied to the ship to propel it along.

For a ship with the *Titanic*'s enormous horsepower, coupled aft of each main engine was the thrust shaft 2ft 3in in diameter with a 9in bore through it. This revolving shaft consisted of 14 collars, arranged with 7 at each

BELOW The completed thrust blocks of the *Britannic*. (UFTM H1946)

end, supported at each end and in the middle by journal bearings. These collars would have been produced by turning them from a larger diameter shaft of forged steel with coupling flanges at either end. The thrust shaft was located in the thrust block, a long cast-iron hollow box shape, rectangular in plan.

The inner bottom of the block held a quantity of oil into which the collars on the shaft dipped. The cast-iron thrust block was in turn firmly bolted down to its seating by bolts through the bottom flanges, and the seating was itself riveted to the tank top. To relieve the holding-down bolts of the shearing stresses encountered, angle iron bar chocks butting against the forward and after end of the thrust block were riveted to the seating. At each end of the block and in the middle was a bearing lined with white metal in which the shaft journals ran.

Two stationary heavy rods of Muntz metal of 2in or 3in diameter, threaded their entire length, were fitted one on either side of the block and secured into cast bosses at each end of the block. These rods were parallel to the thrust shaft and each assembled with a total of 34 brass adjusting nuts.

The collars on the thrust shaft rotated against cast iron thrust 'shoes'. These were fitted into the spaces between the collars and occupied the full width of the thrust block. There were 16 thrust shoes made from cast iron in 'U' form shaped like a horseshoe and faced on both flat sides with white metal and had a thrust area of 3,430in² per engine.

The collars on the thrust shaft transmitted the propeller thrust to the thrust shoes, which in turn transmitted it to the thrust block and then to the hull of the ship. No thrust was actually transmitted to the engine's crankshaft, and the thrust shoes had initially been adjusted during construction so that there was a minimum running clearance between the crank webs and the ends of the main bearings. Ahead thrust was taken up between the forward side of the collars and the after faces of the thrust shoes, the forward face of the shoe taking the thrust when the engine was running astern. The shoes were cast hollow and sea water was circulated through them to prevent overheating of the running surfaces due to friction and any possibility of the white metal melting or 'wiping'.

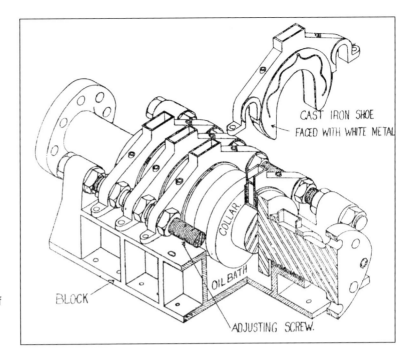

Generally, each side of the horseshoe had a white metal plate with oil grooves attached to the shoe by dowels and recessed cheese-headed bolts so that they could be removed if necessary and a packing 'shim' inserted behind to take up any wear. The forward side of the shoe wore very little and required no more than careful attention. The lower portions of the collars ran in an oil bath while the horseshoe white metal faces were supplied by oil from wick lubricators at their tops.

The LP exhaust turbine had an enclosed thrust block forward with 16 collars of 2ft 8in diameter on a 2ft shaft. The shaft was 4ft 6in long and installed with 17 thrust shoes with a total thrust area of 5,000in².

Lubrication

In slow-running machinery such as the steam reciprocating engines of the *Titanic*, where the speed of rotation was often not more than 75 rev/min, frictional heat was generated at the bearings as a result of heavy pressures acting with low rubbing speeds. With a good lubricant like a mineral oil, the temperature rise necessary to enable radiation and conduction to proceed as fast as heat was generated was moderate, since there were neighbouring masses of chunky machinery with large exposed surfaces to assist in the rapid dissipation of heat. Once thermal equilibrium had been established a

ABOVE Thrust block collar. This simple sketch of a thrust block shows an arrangement with five collars and four 'horseshoe' pads together with its adjusting mechanism. *(Authors' Collections)*

bearing was maintained at an approximately constant running temperature. This may have been too hot to touch, yet, if it was the running temperature for that bearing it would not rise higher unless complications occurred.

One of the anecdotal yarns recounted by engineers concerning the correct running temperature of bearings was the advice: 'Spit on the bearing, if it spits back it's too hot.'

Overheating was not always caused by the working load; bad alignment was also responsible for forces of greater magnitude. If the friction was abnormally great, due to the entrance of grit, insufficient lubrication, or poor bearing metal, the temperature increased so much that before the balance of heat flow had been maintained or restored, seizure had occurred or the lining of the bearing melted ('wiped').

The *Titanic*'s engines were of the 'open' construction type whereby the crossheads, connecting rods, valve rods, crankshafts and bearings were exposed and not enclosed in an oil-tight casing. The open-type engines were lubricated from oil boxes mounted high on the side of the cylinders with lubricating pipes leading down to the various bearings. The flow was controlled either by 'drip feed' or 'automatic drip feed' devices. For the main pistons the water in the steam gave some measure of lubrication. However, information concerning lubrication of the *Titanic*'s main engines is somewhat scant and so it is necessary to draw upon contemporaneous information that was available at the time.

Drip-feed oil boxes had a series of pipes leading down from each box. The pipes in the box extended above the oil level and were fed by strands of worsted, a wick-like material, one end of which was inserted in the tube, the other end being located in the oil by a small lead weight. The oil soaked along the worsted and dripped down the tube, eventually reaching the bearing.

The large end bearings could well have been lubricated through holes in the crank pin journal which were supplied by a forked pipe led through the hollow crank pin from a circular ring of 'U' section which was known as a centrifugal lubricator. The fitting was secured to the side of a crank web and into it oil from the lubrication pipe dripped. The oil was forced centrifugally through the oil pipe in the crank pin and on to the bearing.

The eccentrics of the main engines were similarly fitted with centrifugal lubricators, and the system was also extended to auxiliary engines, which had to work for long periods.

In addition to the normal lubrication supplied through oil pipes to the eccentric sheaves and straps, semi-circular baths were often supplied and secured across the engine bed plate. The baths contained a mixture of oil and water into which the eccentrics dipped, the adhering emulsion then lubricated and cooled these components. The bath was generally replenished by the oil and water draining down the rods from the glands and oil boxes.

As well as the normal oil supply, the guides gained further lubrication from troughs containing oil and water, which were fitted at the bottom of each guide.

The *Titanic* carried 33 greasers, 11 per watch. It was their duty to maintain all oil boxes to the maximum level with oil and ensure other oil reservoirs were topped up and that worsteds were primed at all times and not allowed to dry out.

Generators

Immediately aft of the LP exhaust Turbine Room and located each side of the centre shaft driven by the turbine, were four sets of steam-driven electric generators that supplied power and lighting to the *Titanic*. These were enclosed steam reciprocating engines with their own integral forced lubrication system. Each generator had one high-pressure cylinder of 17in bore and two low-pressure cylinders of 20in bore, all with a combined stroke of 13in. Steam was supplied at 185psi and at a maximum speed of 325 rev/min could produce 580ihp. Exhaust from these was routed either via a service heater or to the auxiliary condenser. The reciprocating prime-movers were directly coupled to a compound wound, continuous current dynamo manufactured by W.H. Allen of Bedford. They produced an output of 4,000A at 100V (400kW), with a total output power of 1600kW.

In addition to the four main generating sets there were two 30kW auxiliary generators located in a recess off the turbine engine room at Saloon Deck level, well above the waterline. They were of compound expansion with a 9in bore high-pressure cylinder and 12in bore low-pressure cylinder with a combined stroke of 5in, and ran at 380rpm. The auxiliary generator sets were connected by means of a separate steam pipe cross-connected to boilers situated in several boiler rooms; in this way the auxiliary generators were available for emergency use should the main sets be out of action.

During the *Titanic*'s sinking, by virtue of their position in the ship, the main generators were not affected by the flooding for as long as the boiler rooms, which were flooded, could keep them supplied with steam.

RIGHT AND BELOW Four 400kW engines and dynamos generated light and electrical power for the entire ship. They were located in the Turbine Engine Room at the after end of the ship.
(UFTM H1533 and H1534)

Chapter Four

Lifeboats

The *Titanic*'s total lifeboat capacity catered only for one-third of her passengers and crew. Out-of-date Board of Trade safety legislation was initially to blame. The *Titanic*'s builders, Harland & Wolff, and owners, White Star, observed the letter of the law when it came to lifeboat provision for the ship, but the delusory belief was that the *Titanic* was unsinkable.

Clinker-built lifeboats from the Cunard liner *Franconia* **(which was being scrapped) were used in scenes for the Rank Organisation's classic 1958 film** *A Night to Remember***, which was shot at Pinewood Studios and on location at Ruislip Lido and Inverkeithing.** *(Authors' Collections)*

Of all the non-structural equipment on board a ship of any size, built for any purpose, the lifeboat must rank among the most important. These small craft are essential to the safety of those on board the parent vessel, and upon them crew and passengers rely for their safe evacuation should the vessel be in danger of foundering.

A ship's lifeboat must be sturdily built and capable of safely transporting its load of survivors over what could be a great distance of ocean; it must be capable of remaining afloat even when partially flooded; it must be able to sail well should the opportunity arise; and it must be able to sustain its passengers with rations of food and water throughout their time adrift.

The lifeboat was essentially a double-ended – or double-bowed – craft. This ensured its seaworthiness because it was less susceptible to broaching by a following sea (being turned and flooded by waves breaking over the exposed side). A 'pointed' stern also offered similar resistance to incoming surf should the boat be beached.

The size of a lifeboat depended upon the type of vessel on which it was carried, and could range from 16ft to 30ft in length. Passenger capacity also dictated the size, with 125cu ft being the bare minimum. The cubic capacity divided by 10 indicated the number of people that could be safely carried in the boat; the cubic capacity was also taken into consideration for the airtight buoyancy tanks incorporated into the structure, which was calculated at 1cu ft for each person carried.

The lifeboat complement for the *Titanic* was:

Twenty boats in all, and of the following dimensions and capacities: 14 wood lifeboats, each 30ft long by 9ft 1in broad by 4ft deep, with a cubic capacity of 655.2cu ft, constructed to carry 65 persons each.

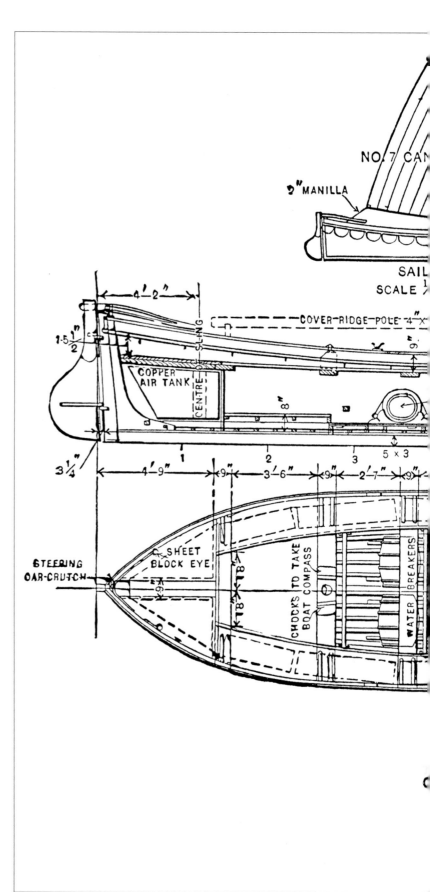

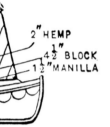

STANDARD SHIP'S LIFE-BOAT.

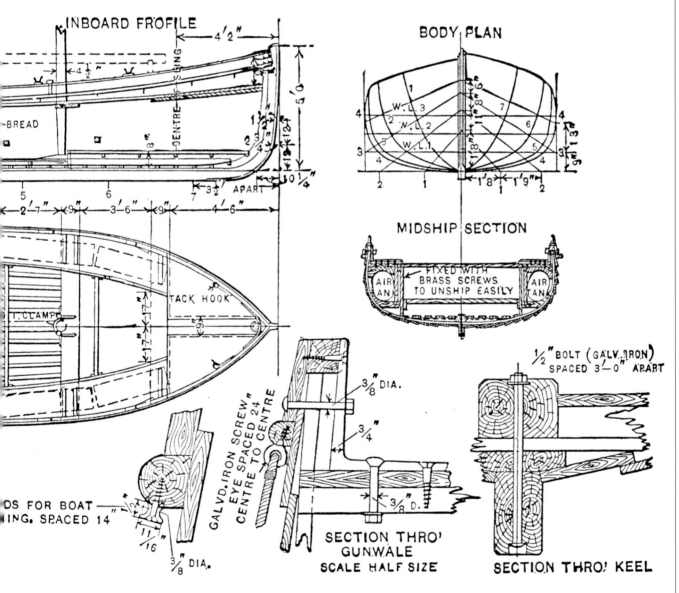

2" HEMP
1"
4½" BLOCK
1½" MANILLA

INBOARD PROFILE

BODY PLAN

MIDSHIP SECTION

FIXED WITH
BRASS SCREWS
TO UNSHIP EASILY

AIR
TAN

AIR
TAN

TACK HOOK

SECTION THRO'
GUNWALE
SCALE HALF SIZE

½" BOLT (GALV. IRON)
SPACED 3'—0" APART

SECTION THRO' KEEL

GALVD. IRON SCREW
EYE SPACED 24"
CENTRE TO CENTRE

DS FOR BOAT
ING. SPACED 14"

There were two emergency boats:

1 wood cutter, 25ft 2in long by 7ft 2in broad
by 3ft deep, with a cubic capacity of
326.6cu ft, constructed to carry 40 persons.
1 wood cutter, 25ft 2in long by 7ft 1in broad
by 3ft deep, with a cubic capacity of
322.1cu ft, constructed to carry 40 persons.

Also, there were the boats additional to Board
of Trade regulations:

4 Engelhardt collapsible boats, 27ft 5in
long by 8ft broad by 3ft deep, with a cubic
capacity of 376.6cu ft, constructed to carry
47 persons each.

Although the law would oblige the 'Olympics'
to have a lifeboat capacity for 990 persons,
including the collapsible boat capacity, the
Titanic's lifeboat capacity was calculated
at 1,327.9cu ft for 1,178 persons. At her
potential capacity *Titanic* could, according to
the passenger certificate (which differed from
the technical specification) issued to 'a foreign-
going steamship', carry 2,603 passengers as
well as 944 crew – some 3,547 'souls' in total.

The Olympic Class had been designed with
the possibility of changes in safety legislation
in mind. These ships could be speedily
converted to carry up to 68 lifeboats when

those anticipated changes became a legal
requirement. Welin's double-acting quadrant
davits, which were already installed on the
'Olympics', could be swung inboard as well as
out in order to pick up additional lifeboats which
might be stowed inboard of those already fitted.

However, until the existing legislation
stipulating that a ship of 10,000 gross tons
or more (which was a large vessel at the time
the legislation was enacted) should carry 16
boats could be changed, the Olympic Class
was destined to carry 14 30ft boats, each
with a capacity of 60–65 persons; two 25ft
emergency boats, each capable of nominally
carrying 33 persons (40 on the White Star
specification); and four Engelhardt collapsible
boats constructed with planked, clinker-built
bottoms, on which were mounted canvas sides,
supported by foldable frame stiffeners which
could be raised, designed to carry 47.

The latter boats – of which two were stowed
alongside the two emergency boats placed
forward of the two sets of three 30ft boats
at the fore end of the Boat Deck, port and
starboard, and two placed atop the officers'
quarters – enabled the 'Olympics' to exceed
the *legal* requirement of boats carried by a
margin of 25 per cent. This gave a life-saving
capacity of over 1,178 people, which, because
of the watertight design of the 'Olympics', was

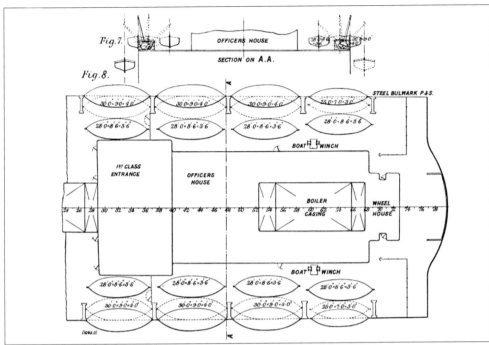

LEFT This diagram from Axel Welin's 1912 INA paper 'The Arrangement of Boat Installations of Modern Ships' shows proposed numbers and arrangement of lifeboats on the Olympic Class just prior to another reduction by the White Star Line. *(Authors' Collections)*

BELOW As yet unpainted during fitting out, the Welin davits on board *Olympic* are shown with boats already stowed. Note the rope guards under the boats to prevent any accidents occurring to passengers and crew during heavy seas. *(TopFoto)*

Welin Quadrant Davit

The new Welin-type davit was designed to forcibly swing outboard (or inboard) by the incorporation of a gear-toothed quadrant on the lower edge of the davit, set between the arms of the split davit arm that formed an inverted 'Y', which constituted the base of each davit. This moveable toothed arc (backed by a supporting flange moulded on the inward facing side) then engaged with a similarly castellated but straight rack (the teeth being flanged on the outward facing side) fastened securely to the deck.

The davits and frames were forged from high-quality cast steel and, on a single-acting davit, the tensile strength of the steel was not less than 60,000lb/sq in and not in excess of 72,000lb/sq in (the double-acting type was presumably of a similar specification).

The davit was set in motion by rotating a horizontal trapezoidal screw-threaded shaft made of 'Tobin' – a type of phosphor bronze – set between the uprights of the deck-mounted frame and kept securely in place with the aid of a tie bar. This also acted as a sliding bar for a screw block (a double-bored collar looking rather like a short but oversized double-barreled shotgun) about 10in long, one bore being threaded to suit the 'Tobin' shaft and the other plain-bored to slide along the tie bar. The threaded shaft was supported and restrained at both ends on hardened steel collars by the fixed frame of the davit. Both shafts were protected by a flanged plate.

This double-bored collar that linked both threaded shaft and tie-bar was moulded with a central shaft placed at right angles and horizontal to the collar. This shaft (acting much like the axle of a wheel) passed through a round hole moulded at the pivot point in the davit's centre of rotation (at the centre – or hub – of the quadrant) and was held in place on the outward side of the davit by a collar that acted as a retaining flange. When the davit was operated this collar, rotating about its axle, would then remain horizontal whilst the davit arm turned about its arc of rotation, much like a wheel.

The swan-necked davit itself acted as an elongated spoke.

The rotation of the shaft was achieved by attaching a cranked handle with a hollow female square keyway in the handle matching a square male key on the shaft's inboard end which, on being turned, caused the shaft to rotate.

On the application of the cranking handle the davit arm was thus moved outboard, the action of the quadrant automatically lifting the lifeboat from its seating chocks. The davit could be extended quite far outboard, helping to overcome the effects of a greater amount of listing than could be sustained by a round-bar davit.

In the case of a Welin double-acting davit, when the handle rotation was reversed the davit moved inboard to pick up a boat stowed in tandem. The Welin double-acting type of davits, which were described as 'providing the most expeditious and satisfactory means for launching ships' boats', could be 'reversed' inboard to an angle sufficient to attach its tackle to that second lifeboat.

The design and operation of the Welin Quadrant (or, more correctly, semi-quadrant as a lifeboat was lifted through an arc of a circle created by the quadrant form of the davit's lower end) davits was an ingeniously simple one, which simplified the launching and greatly reduced the time that it took to launch the lifeboat into the water, an operation which could be undertaken, if need be, by two men – one on each davit.

On the Olympic Class there were two types of double-acting davit. Although both had single frames, the davits placed at both ends of each bank of lifeboats only had a single davit operated by one 'Tobin' shaft, while the other type had two davits, one placed on either side of the frame; both davits were operated by their own shaft and sleeve. Although this arrangement was primarily to save space it also meant that only one of two adjacent boats could be manoeuvred at any one time.

To change operational movement from one davit to the other, a switch-over gearing was built into the frame below the cranking mechanism.

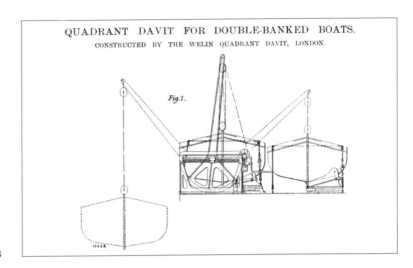

QUADRANT DAVIT FOR DOUBLE-BANKED BOATS.
CONSTRUCTED BY THE WELIN QUADRANT DAVIT, LONDON.

Fig.1.

considered more than sufficient until the new regulations came into force. The collapsibles on top of the officers' quarters were intended to be moved to the davits (once these were vacated by the decked lifeboats), although this manoeuvre could not be performed without difficulty as the boats were not 'under davits' as were their counterparts stowed alongside the emergency boats.

In addition to the ship's boats, 48 lifebuoys were provided as were 3,455 lifebelts for adults and 300 for children.

The 30ft Harland & Wolff boats had a breadth of 9ft 1in and a depth of 4ft. By multiplying the product of the main dimensions by a factor of 0.6 (this allowed for the narrowing of the ends) and dividing the result by 10, it gave the recommended carrying capacity of the boat – 65 persons.

The 25-footers were carried forward port and starboard just aft of the Bridge. They were designated as emergency boats, which could be quickly lowered, for example in the event of a man overboard, and for such a purpose they were kept slung and lashed outboard.

To comply with the expected changes in the Board of Trade regulations, consideration had also been given by January 1912 to supply a further 12 open lifeboats of 27ft 5in in length; 12 decked boats of the same length; 8 open 29ft boats; 14 additional 30ft boats (but with a lesser beam of 3ft 7in as opposed to the 4ft beam of those already fitted); and 2 decked boats of 28ft length. According to the notebook of Thomas Andrews (the shipyard manager in charge of design), these changes would ensure

RIGHT For 'long shots' in the film *A Night to Remember* the Royal Mail liner (latterly troopship) *Asturias*, then being scrapped in Scotland, was used to great effect. The liner's own steel boats were used in these scenes, but with 'clinker' lines painted on them. (Authors' Collections)

a total of 68 boats with a combined capacity for 3,538 persons, just in excess of the number of people on board the *Titanic*. It would be assumed that once the full complement of boats was fitted within range of the davits, the collapsible boats could be dispensed with. Although this anticipated increase in the number of boats would meet legal requirements – and the boat capacity would exceed the ships' total complement – it would only be effective if all the boats could be got away from the liner and each one was fully loaded.

As the Olympic Class was considered to be 'practically unsinkable', the use of the lifeboats was anticipated mainly as a means of transporting people from the damaged ship to the vessel rendering assistance. In fact, normal use of the lifeboats was for crew practice in regulation demonstrations of efficiency and, in the case of the emergency boats, for rapid deployment should a 'man overboard' event arise.

Construction

Ships' lifeboats were built by skilled boat builders, with fittings made by coppersmiths and blacksmiths, who took great pride in their workmanship and a satisfaction in the quality of the materials being used. Great care was taken that a ship's lifeboat was built without stress to the materials used, and that all component parts lay in place 'naturally'.

BELOW Boat building at John I. Thornycroft's yard in Southampton. *(Authors' Collections)*

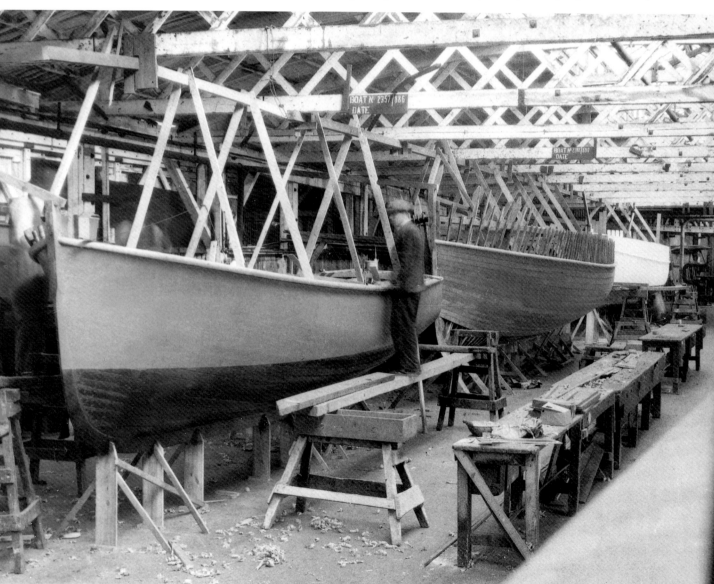

Keel, hog, risings, planking, rubbers and gunwales were worked in one length to provide a continuity of strength that would resist the bending moments to which the boat would become subjected.

Experienced boat builders gave much thought to the practice of their skills and often developed methods that became idiosyncratic to their locale, although a quality product was the aim of reputable boat builders wherever they worked throughout the country. The boat-building shop at Harland & Wolff had its own preferences on which timbers and other materials were to be used, but the following description gives an insight into the choices available.

Class 1A lifeboats were of wooden construction with planking arranged in clinker fashion – or clincher (sometimes called lapstrake) – and copper-clenched. This style of boat-building, in use since Saxon and Viking times, had the advantage over other types of construction in being reasonably quick and economic to achieve as well as being easily repaired.

Although teak and mahogany were often chosen, these particular woods were generally used on lifeboats of ships that sailed to the tropics. A simplistic guide was 'northern timbers for northern waters' (where the Olympic Class was designed to operate) and tropical timbers for tropical waters.

For the *Titanic*'s lifeboats:

> . . . keels were elm. The stems and stern posts were of oak. They were all clinker-built of yellow pine, double-fastened with copper nails, clinched [clenched] over roves. The timbers were of elm, spaced about 9 inches apart, and the seats pitch pine secured with galvanized iron double-knees. The buoyancy tanks in the lifeboats were of 18oz copper, and of capacity to meet the Board of Trade requirements.

A well-built boat had a very pleasing appearance – almost wooden 'sculptures' imbued with an organic feel – with a clean sweep of line enhanced by a graceful sheer of ½in to the foot, a practical feature that provided additional buoyancy and which enabled the ends of the craft to comfortably rise to an oncoming sea. A good sheer was also aesthetically pleasing to those passengers cognisant with the niceties of such standards as they promenaded along the Boat Deck. To the uninitiated traveller the boats were ignored, overlooked or considered as unnecessary hindrances that interrupted their view of the sea.

Inspection

Charles Lightoller, the Second Officer of *Titanic*, recalled the lifeboat inspection by the Board of Trade's Captain Clark while the ship was in Southampton and being readied for her maiden voyage:

BELOW **A rare surviving double-acting davit of the type installed on the *Titanic* in store at a location in England. Note the hole about which the davit 'wheel' pivoted during operation.** *(David Williams)*

Board of Trade surveys were carried out to everyone's satisfaction. Lifeboats and all life-saving equipment tested, exercised and passed . . . Being a new ship, and the biggest in the world, even more scrupulous care was exercised than is usual or applies to a ship on her settled run. The Board of Trade Surveyor, Captain Clerk [sic] certainly lived up to his reputation of being the best-cursed B.O.T. representative in the South of England at that time. Many small details that another surveyor would have taken in his stride, accepting the statement of the officer concerned, was not good enough for Clark – he must see everything and himself check every item that concerned the survey. He would not accept anyone's word as sufficient, and got heartily cursed in consequence. He did his job . . . he did it thoroughly.

Perhaps Captain Clark's thoroughness in his inspection of the boats was driven by a knowledge that the BoT's regulations were woefully out of date and an awareness that White Star, through its Olympic Class, had stolen a march on the Board by reducing the original number of intended boats to the Board's minimum, but adding the extra four collapsibles (although these flouted the rules by not being 'under davits') as a sop. The inspector's thoroughness possibly hid an anxiety about the lack of boats.

It was a time for holding one's breath until the outdated regulations could be changed and enforced.

BELOW The sad aftermath of a great tragedy. The only parts of the *Titanic* to reach New York were her lifeboats, seen here after being landed from the *Carpathia*. Both 30ft and 25ft 2in ('Emergency') boats are shown, clearly revealing the details of their construction.
(Authors' Collections)

Boat building

I n contrast to the deafening clamour that typified the heavy industrial engineering might of an active, early 20th-century shipyard, the atmosphere in a boat shop was one of comparative tranquillity, permeated perhaps by the low-staccato of ball-pein hammers clenching soft copper nails.

The aromatic smell of finely shaved and drilled woods pervaded the air as craftsmen – *the* boat builders – plied their trade, their honed and sharpened tools proud extensions of their skilled hands.

Although not comprehensive of all stages of boat building, these photographs from the Lyme Regis Boat Building Academy in Dorset give a flavour of the pride that boat builders still take in their ancient craft.

The boat builders of Harland & Wolff took a similar pride in the lifeboats they built for the *Titanic*, a pride boosted by the fact that their handiwork had saved over 700 lives; a pride shaken that insufficient of their work had been provided to save many, many, more.

(All photographs © Lyme Regis Boat Building Academy, Dorset)

1 Keel, stem, and stern are erected in readiness for the moulds to be applied.

2 Fashioning a stem knee with a spokeshave.

3 The apron is secured to the stem.

4 Moulds are set in place on the keel assembly and steadied by stays connected to an overhead beam, in readiness for planking to begin.

5 The careful fitting of the garboard strakes determines the lay of subsequent planks.

6 The hood-end of this garboard strake is feathered and fitted.

7 A spiling batten is clamped in place in readiness for lifting the shape of the next plank.

8 Having marked details for the shape of the next plank on to the spiling batten, the shape is transferred to a board of planking material.

9 Test-fitting the next plank in readiness for cutting the gerald and fitting the hood end.

10 Planking is now complete and ready for the fitting of the stiffening timbers.

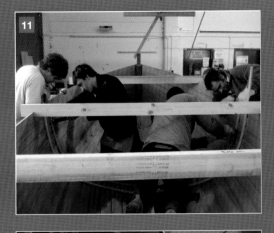

11 Timbers are taken straight from the steam box and bent into place.

12 The timber is held steady with a dolly while a clenching nail is driven through the still hot timber. Once the timbers are cool, roves are placed over the nail points, which are then trimmed off and clenched over the rove.

13 The planking has been pre-drilled and clenching nails are fitted in readiness for driving through the steamed timbers ('hot nailing'). The lines of a Viking longship can almost be seen!

14 Timbering is almost complete.

15 Timbers and part of the gunwale are in place.

16 Planks, sheer strake, rubbers and gunwales are all in place.

17 Sole boards protect the craft from hard wear and tear.

Chapter Five

View from the Bridge

A ship the size of the *Titanic* was navigated by only seven officers (also known as Deck Officers or Mates), overseen by the Master of the ship, Captain Edward J. Smith, often referred to as 'the Commander' in White Star Line literature.

Titanic's bridge superstructure, viewed from the foredeck.
(Topfoto)

In common with other merchant vessels, *Titanic*'s junior deck officers operated the traditional watch system. The Third and Fifth Officers 'stood' the 4:00–8:00am watch; noon–4:00pm; 6:00–8:00pm (second dog watch); and midnight–4:00am. The Fourth and Sixth Officers 'stood' the midnight–4:00am; 8:00am–noon; 4:00–6:00pm (first dog watch), and 8.00pm–midnight. In this manner the watch roster was continually rotated for the junior officers.

The three senior officers worked the same hours every day. The Chief Officer 'stood' the 2:00–6:00am/pm watches; the First Officer 10:00–2:00pm/am and the Second Officer 6:00–10:00pm/am. Two officers at a time 'stood' watch; the more senior was known as the Officer of the Watch (OOW). The latter had a great many duties in addition to plotting the ship's course and manning the Bridge. He was required constantly to check that the ship's navigation (side) lights and masthead lights were kept burning. With the *Titanic*'s electrical system this could be checked by small pilot lamps that kept aglow on the Bridge itself so long as the circuits to the main lights were in order. The OOW would monitor the compass and ship's heading and, along with the barometer pressure and sea temperature, enter their readings in the ship's log at regular intervals. He also took sights on the sun at midday and stars at night, besides always keeping a sharp lookout. When quiet on the Bridge one of the officers would do deck rounds, checking rigging, the correct stowage of lifeboat pulleys, and that the lifeboats' canvas covers were in place.

Ship's time was marked by bells which were struck on the half-hour. At the end of eight bells – the full watch – the round began over again. Thus 8 o'clock, 12 o'clock and 4 o'clock were all eight bells, 4:30 was one bell, 5 o'clock two bells, and so on. On the *Titanic*, the ship's bell was hung on the foremast where a lookout was stationed in the crow's-nest. It was often customary for the lookout to receive his cue from the Bridge where a smaller bell was struck every half hour, after which the lookout sounded his larger tocsin.

The Chief Officer was also responsible for organising the deck department crew under the boatswain, and navigation and stowage of any cargo along with the deck gear, including

Edward John Smith – Captain of the *Titanic*

Edward John Smith was born on 27 January 1850 in Hanley, which is now part of Stoke-on-Trent in Staffordshire. He started work at 14 as a steam-hammer operator in a foundry and became apprenticed on a sailing ship, under the command of his half-brother, sailing to the Far East, the Americas and home.

On leaving sail, EJ (as he was known), now a Master Mariner, joined the *Celtic* of the White Star Line as Fourth Officer in 1880. Promotions followed on other ships until 1887 when he achieved his first White Star command as temporary Captain of *Republic* before reverting to First Officer on *Britannic*.

Gaining his Extra Master's Certificate in 1888, EJ was promoted to Captain and joined the Royal Naval Reserve as Lieutenant Edward J. Smith RNR. Captaincy of several White Star ships followed until he was given command of the *Majestic*, staying on her for nearly nine years and taking her to Cape Colony during the Boer War, for which he was awarded the Transport Medal. Becoming known as 'the millionaires' Captain', he rose to become Commodore of the Line, taking White Star ships on their first voyages, including the mighty *Olympic*. Once he had taken *Titanic* on her maiden voyage it had been mooted that EJ would retire, but it was rumoured that he intended to stay on to take the third sister of the trio on her first trip.

Two days after sailing from Southampton on 10 April, warnings of ice in the shipping lanes began to be received. As a precaution Captain Smith delayed a change of course that would bring the ship on a heading for New York at a position known as 'The Corner' at the 47th Meridian, a delay that would take the ship about 25 miles further south with the intention of circumnavigating the ice.

After dinner on the evening of the 14th, Captain Smith briefly went to the Bridge and ordered that he be called if conditions became doubtful. At 11.40pm he rushed on to the Bridge, the bells of closing watertight doors indicating that something was wrong. The *Titanic* had struck an iceberg a glancing blow.

Edward John Smith.
(Authors' Collections)

Consulting with the ship's designer, Thomas Andrews, Captain Smith realised that his ship had less than two hours to live. His orders over the next hour were to send out radio calls for assistance; uncover the lifeboats; put women and children first into the boats and lower away; fire rockets to attract assistance; issue the officers with revolvers in case they were needed; and, finally, to abandon ship.

Captain Smith's final moments are unclear. Did he suffer a breakdown and did command evaporate? Was he on the Bridge when the forward funnel fell? Did he swim to an upturned lifeboat with a child in his arms? His last moments are one of *Titanic*'s mysteries.

deck games. He would be responsible for the deck department administration and overseeing the watch rota. A majority of his time could be spent on day work as well.

During times of stand-by, manoeuvring in and out of port or in thick fog, the Master would be present on the Bridge and other officers would be stationed on the Docking Bridge astern, and also on the forecastle alongside the windlass, which was operated in an emergency by the ship's carpenter.

During her trials in Belfast Lough on 1 April 1912, the *Titanic* achieved a cruising speed of 21kt and during a manoeuvre to bring her to a halt, she went from Full Speed Ahead, with the LP turbine engaged, to Full Speed Astern with the turbine disengaged to a stop, in 850yd. Since there was no astern blading on the turbine she was normally manoeuvred as a twin-screw vessel.

One of the anomalies of the ship's steering practice was that it was White Star's policy to use antiquated sailing ship orders for steering up until the First World War, and this was highlighted following the *Titanic* disaster. As the vast majority of White Star's navigating officers were apprenticed in sail, in the early days custom and practice was probably expected. In these orders, the steering was done by the tiller (the horizontal beam at the top of the rudder post). For example, if the ship's heading was desired to be full over to port, the order was given 'Hard to starboard'. In this the ship's wheel (helm) was spun to port, the tiller moved to starboard, and the rudder and ship's heading was also to port. It was not until 1 January 1931 that most nations began to adopt the practice of relating helm orders to the rudder and no longer to the tiller. Thus an order of say 'starboard 20' meant turning the wheel, the rudder and the ship's heading to starboard.

During the night of the collision with an iceberg it is believed that the *Titanic* was ploughing ahead through a calm sea at about 21½kt.

Control of steering gear

The steering gear was controlled from the Navigating Bridge by Brown telemotors, and from the Docking Bridge by mechanical means. The telemotor cylinders

BELOW The internal arrangement of the *Titanic*'s bridge. *(Authors' Collections)*

were placed near the steering engines and were connected by levers and shafting to the steam control valves on the engines. The control valve on each engine was fitted with a Brown's type 'economic' valve which automatically shut off the steam when the engine was at rest and thus prevented leakage of steam into the cylinders. The precise position of the rudder at any moment was shown by means of an electric helm indicator situated on the Bridge.

Navigation and wireless equipment

The Navigating Bridge, from which the *Titanic* was controlled, was situated at the forward end of the boat deck, so that the navigating officer had a clear view ahead. At the centre of the Bridge was the wheelhouse containing the telemotor control wheel by which the ship was steered, with a standard compass immediately in front. Forward of the wheelhouse were the engine room, docking and steering telegraphs, and loud-speaking telephones to various stations. In the bridge shelter or chart room adjoining was the watertight door controller, the submarine-signal receiver, the helm indicator and the master clocks. Down aft on the Poop Deck was a Docking Bridge for use when the vessel was docking or turning in a confined space.

The Wireless Telegraphy equipment consisted of a Marconi 1½kW standard ship set. The Marconi apparatus was situated in the Marconi Room at the after end of the officers' accommodation on the boat deck. The two parallel aerial wires required for the system extended between the *Titanic*'s masts. They were kept as high as possible and were fastened to light booms, the latter of which were attached to the masts. From the aerial wires, connecting wires led down to instruments in the Marconi Room. There were two complete sets of apparatus, one for transmitting and one for receiving messages; the latter had been placed in a sound-proof chamber built into a corner of the room. This equipment was operated by two Marconi wireless officers.

ABOVE A young admirer chats with Captain Smith. *(The Wonder Book of Ships)*

LEFT Captain Smith looking over the side of the *Titanic*'s docking bridge when she was moored at Queenstown. *(Fr Browne SJ Collection)*.

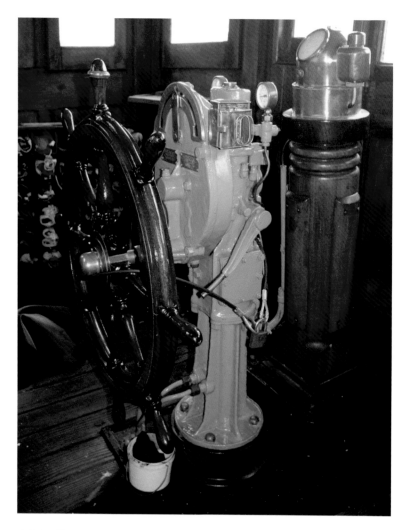

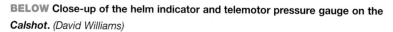

ABOVE The ship's wheel, telemotor housing and binacle in the wheelhouse of the Southampton tender *Calshot*. *(David Williams)*

BELOW Close-up of the helm indicator and telemotor pressure gauge on the *Calshot*. *(David Williams)*

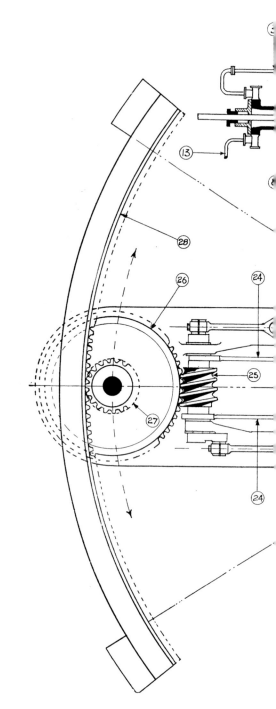

Brown's Patent Telemotor and Steering Gear

1. Transmitting cylinder operated by hand steering wheel.
2. Pipe from top end of cylinder.
3. Pipe from bottom end of cylinder.
4. Rack connected to piston of transmitter cylinder.
5. By-pass valve for putting both ends of cylinder in communication, if required.
6. By-pass annular space in cylinder to bring gear and rudder into midship position.

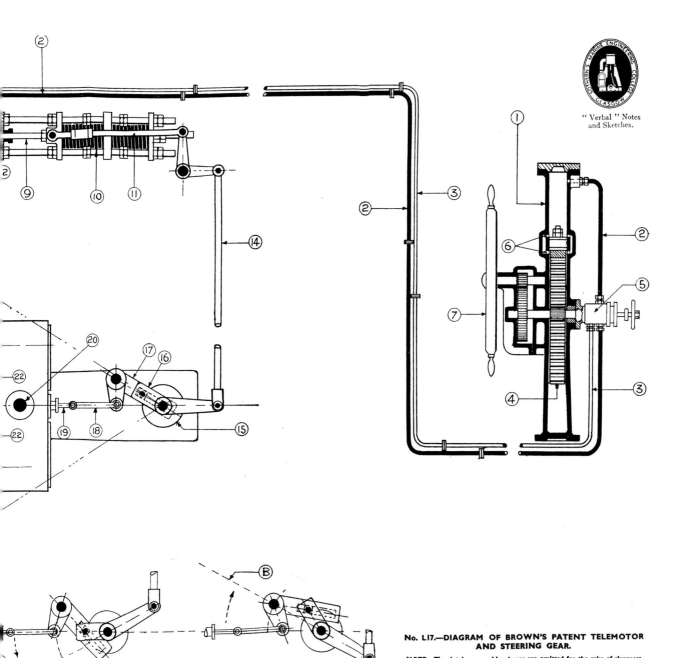

No. L17.—DIAGRAM OF BROWN'S PATENT TELEMOTOR AND STEERING GEAR.

NOTE.—The clutch gear and hand gear are omitted for the sake of clearness.

7. Hand steering wheel.
8. Receiving cylinder placed aft near steering engine.
9. Piston rod acting on crosshead and springs.
10. Springs.
11. Links from crosshead to bell crank of control valve rod.
12. Pipe and non-return valve connecting to charging tank.
13. Pipe connecting to hand pump.
14. Rod for telemotor gear to control valve gear.
15. Rudder stock.
16. Slotted lever of hunting or cut-off gear.
17. Bell crank arm of hunting gear.
18. Link connecting bell crank to control valve spindle.
19. Control valve spindle.
20. Steam inlet branch.
21. Control valve casing.
22. Piston valves of engine.
23. Cylinder glands.
24. Connecting rods.
25. Worm on engine crankshaft.
26. Worm wheel.
27. Pinion wheel gearing with teeth on quadrant rack.
28. Rack quadrant with teeth.

OPPOSITE A contemporary photograph showing the interior of the radio room of an Atlantic liner. During daytime the range of the *Titanic*'s Marconi radio equipment was about 500 miles; at night this increased to over 1500 miles. *(Illustrated London News)*

RIGHT Marconi radio operators Jack Phillips (left) and colleague, photographed aboard the White Star liner *Adriatic*. As Chief Wireless Telegraphist, Jack Phillips lost his life on the *Titanic* staying at his post to near the very end, sending out SOS messages. *(Father Browne Collection/Getty Images)*

BELOW The Marconi radio operator at work in his radio room on the Bridge Deck of the *Titanic*. *(Illustrated London News)*

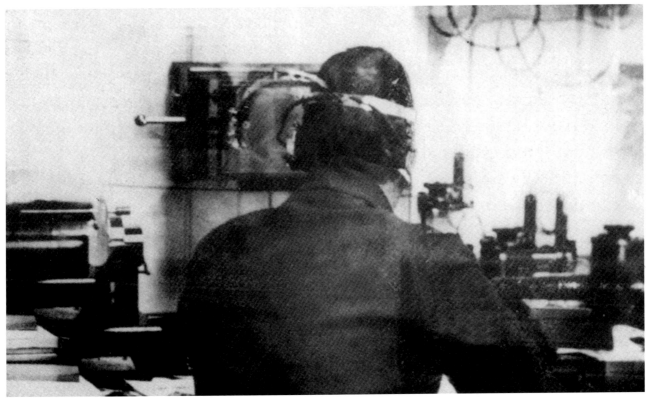

Chapter Six

Engineer's View

In overall charge of the Engine and Boiler Rooms, ancillary equipment and all engineering personnel was the Chief Engineer. He was identified by four gold braid rings around each sleeve, with purple velvet between them to denote the Engineering Branch. During the *Titanic*'s era, engineers at sea were not considered as officers. The *Titanic*'s Chief Engineer, Joseph Bell, did not survive the sinking.

A scene from the film *A Night to Remember*, depicting *Titanic*'s Engine Room in operation. *(Authors' Collections)*

The duties of a ship's Chief Engineer at the time of the *Titanic* were many and varied. He was obliged to carry out the orders of the Captain and he would be held accountable for the discipline and good order of the Engine Department. If orders were received which, in his opinion, would endanger the boilers or machinery, he had to explain this to the Captain and report to the Superintendent Engineer ashore. He was responsible for the efficient management and working of the machinery and boilers and of the steam, electric, hydraulic, refrigerating, disinfecting and other equipment.

It was his duty to visit the Engine Department regularly. He had to be present in the Engine Room when the ship was entering or leaving harbour, or passing through intricate channels. When in a UK port, he was responsible for seeing that the Engine Room, stokehold and any cargo machinery was properly attended and that sufficient engineers, competent to deal with any emergency, were always on board.

When a Chief Engineer was appointed to a ship he took over from his predecessor all fuel, stores, spare gear, tools, books, papers and gauges belonging to his department, the signed receipts for which would be forwarded to the Superintendent Engineer ashore.

The Chief Engineer was expected to understand the principles and construction of the machinery and boilers. He was supplied with full instructions for all the various installations, so that he could direct the engineers and others under his charge and ensure that the department was run at maximum efficiency. He also checked that the junior engineers, especially those who kept watches, were fully acquainted with the construction and all aspects of the engines and boilers, in order to perform their duties.

The Chief Engineer would personally inspect the engines to check that they were in good repair and properly adjusted. He had to see that the boilers and mountings were also in good condition and would examine the boilers internally before they were filled with water. After the boilers were filled and getting ready to raise steam, he had to inspect them in the presence of the Second Engineer and the Engineer of the Watch, to ensure that the water in the gauge glass on each boiler was at the proper height. Simultaneously, he had to examine all the blow-down and salinometer cocks or valves to satisfy himself that they were all properly shut. The operation of blowing through the gauge glass cocks had to be repeated as soon as sufficient steam was generated in the boilers, in order to make sure that no water was lost by leakage due to cocks or valves not having been properly shut after the boilers had been filled.

Only when the Chief Engineer was satisfied that the engines were operational in all respects – having been warmed through and moved over both centres, ahead and astern – would he report to the Captain that they were ready for sea. When the stand-by bell was rung to indicate that the engines were ready, the Chief Engineer had to ensure that all the senior, intermediate and junior engineers and the Engine Room crew on watch were at their stations. On leaving or approaching any port abroad, and in all home waters, the Chief or Second Engineer would be in charge of the engine room, and double watches of engineers were kept. The stand-by had to be maintained for two hours by the watch last off duty and the following two hours by the next watch coming on duty. It was the job of the senior engineer working the telegraph to observe the actual movement of the engines in order to make sure that the movement corresponded with the order from the Bridge.

In addition to the maintenance and efficient operation of the machinery, the Chief Engineer was expected to keep the Boiler and Engine Room bilges clean and free from any accumulation of oil, water, oily water and coal dust. He was held personally responsible for the condition of the bilges and would frequently inspect them. Engineers in charge of watches were instructed to keep the bilge-water levels as low as possible, and to enter the depth of water in the Engine Room Rough Log Book (see Administrative Duties).

Further responsibilities included ensuring that all sluice valves, cocks and watertight doors in the Engine Department, both on bulkheads and coal bunkers, were in good working order. When coal trimmers moved from one bunker to another, the watertight doors had to be closed after they left.

All material that had been used for wiping the engines, or in any other way smeared with oil, had to be destroyed immediately and not left lying around the engine and boiler spaces for fear of spontaneous combustion. Cans and stone jars containing oil and other inflammable stores were never stowed in a warm place.

The Chief Engineer was held responsible for the running order of the winches, hydraulic gear, windlass and capstans, steering gear, telemotors, steam-driven generators, electric light, electric wiring, and electric motors, fans and bells, steam fire annihilators, steam warming pipes and all steam connections with the galley, galley appliances, bathrooms and refrigerating machinery, as well as the distilling apparatus. He would personally see that all working parts were properly oiled and worked not less than once a week and when this was done an entry was made in the Engine Room Log Book.

Another of his tasks was to ensure that all his men cleaned their quarters, appeared at muster at hours appointed by the Captain and washed their clothes when at sea on specified days.

Management and working of the engines

It was the Chief Engineer's responsibility to ensure that all his engineers on watch were competent to work the engines in an emergency, according to the orders from the Bridge, until he could reach the Engine Room to assist them. The engineers on watch were expected to supervise all the men under their charge, including those working on the shafting and boilers. They could not leave the Engine Room and boiler spaces during their watch unless relieved by another engineer. Should engineers on watch discover any defect or breakdown to any part of the machinery or boilers they had to summon the Chief Engineer immediately. In the meantime, they had to take such steps necessary to prevent an accident.

After the fires were lit in the boilers and the temperature in them was sufficiently high, all communications to the engines would be opened, so that air could be expelled from the pipes and cylinders and the engines warmed up gradually. Before warming through the main engines, the circulating water pumps would be started up to send water through the condensers and would be kept running until the main engines were fully under way. This means of circulation would also be used when the main engines were stopped at sea or entering ports.

Great care had to be paid to the lubrication of the engine's working parts to ensure they were maintained in smooth working order without excessive heating. Should the latter occur, the Chief Engineer was immediately summoned.

Whenever possible while away from the UK, the Chief Engineer would employ the engineers and men under him in examining and repairing the ship's machinery. If any serious defects or flaws were detected, he would inform the Captain and discuss the options. Unless there was some immediate danger, or a mechanical breakdown was imminent, he was, in consultation with the Captain, expected to use his own discretion as to the best means of dealing with the problem in order to bring the ship safely home. At the same time he had to enter the defect in the Engine Room Log Book and report the facts to the Superintendent Engineer.

ABOVE The Engine Room interior of a typical steam ship in the 1920s. In the foreground is the thrust block, which is made up of five pods that had to have constant lubrication. *(Topham Picturepoint/TopFoto)*

RIGHT This stokehold photograph of firemen on an earlier ship shows the hot, dark, coal dust laden atmosphere in which they worked. The taking of this photograph must have provided a short respite from their back-breaking, sweaty task. *(Denis Steele)*

The Engine Room watch could not be relieved until after the engineers coming on watch had checked that:

1. The engines were working properly.
2. All bearings were running cool.
3. Water in all boilers was at the correct level.
4. The steam was at the proper pressure.
5. A sufficient quantity of coal was left on the stokehold plates in front of each boiler.

If anything was amiss, the Chief Engineer had to visit the Engine Room and see that it was in proper order before he could allow the watch to be relieved. He would enter any case of neglect or lack of skill in the Engine Room Log Book.

When the main engines were finished with, care would be taken to ascertain that the main inlet and discharge valves were properly closed.

Management of boilers

The Chief Engineer had to ensure that all his engineers were fully acquainted with the connections of the boilers, and understood their use and working. He had to be very particular, when raising steam, to see that the fires were lit at least 18 to 24 hours before it was required, so that steam would be generated slowly to avoid damage to the boilers, which might otherwise suffer from sudden expansion. If, in cases of emergency, steam had to be raised more rapidly, every possible precaution had to be taken to prevent damage from unequal expansion. In all such cases, the circumstances were reported to the Superintendent Engineer.

During the process of raising steam, attention was paid to the steam pressure gauges in both the Boiler and Engine Rooms to see that all indicated alike. It was the Chief Engineer's duty to instruct the engineers in charge of the different watches as to the height of water to be maintained in the boilers.

It was recommended that the steam pressure in the boilers when leaving or entering ports should never be allowed to get higher than from 20 to 30psi under the load upon the safety valves, but the Chief Engineer would be guided by circumstances. If the engines were stopped suddenly, the safety valves would at once be eased using the hand gear to ensure they were free and in good order.

The Chief Engineer personally took the density of the water in each boiler at least once every 24 hours and the engineers on watch took it every four hours, and the findings were entered in the Engine Room 'Rough Log Book'. If any defect or derangement occurred in the feed pumps, feed valves, or the feed pipes, affecting the level of the water in any of the boilers, the engineers of the watch were expected to take the necessary precautions to prevent damage to the boiler and summon the Chief Engineer. Water was never allowed to get out of sight in the gauge glass without the fires being immediately drawn and the Chief Engineer called.

When a ship was away from the UK and in harbour for any length of time, the boiler tubes and ashpits, as well as the inside of the boilers, were cleaned. If any decay, wasting away, or pitting of the plates was discovered, the area was washed out and coated with zinc paint or Portland Cement made up with fresh water and applied as a whitewash. The Chief Engineer examined the boilers before and after scaling and submitted a report to the Superintendent Engineer on each occasion.

At the end of the voyage, after the fires had been drawn, boilers would not be blown down; instead, if time permitted, the water would be allowed to cool and run into the bilges to be pumped overboard.

Propellers

When a ship was dry-docked, it was the Chief Engineer's duty to examine the boss, blades and nuts that secured the propeller and to check the shaft for wear with a 'wear down gauge'. When the shaft was drawn during a survey, the soundness of the brass liners on the shaft and the lignum vitae bearings in the stern tube would be tested and a report sent to the Superintendent Engineer. The zinc plates (sacrificial anodes) in the vicinity of the propellers were also examined and renewed as required.

Electric light

The generator (prime mover and dynamo) and the spare gear came under the control of the Chief Engineer, who was responsible for the proper working of the electrical installation and for it being kept clean and in good order. The electrical engineering staff were accountable to the Chief Engineer.

Fuel consumption

As the largest and by far the most important item in the company's expenditure was fuel, the most rigid economy was exercised in its use. The directors considered that by constant attention on the part of not only the Captain and Chief Engineer but also the other engineers, that by careful stoking and judicious treatment of the fires, keeping the water in the boilers at the proper level and the steam at a uniformly regular pressure, a considerable saving in the consumption of fuel could be made.

Every endeavour was made to economise on fuel whenever circumstances permitted. This was done by working the expansion gear and regulating the revolutions to achieve the required speed without causing the ship to arrive at port behind time, as maintaining the scheduled timetable was essential to the service. The Captain and Chief Engineer were expected to consult with a view to reducing fuel consumption to the lowest limit possible, depending on the circumstances of the voyage.

Administrative duties

The Chief Engineer was held responsible for fulfilling all the administrative duties of the Engineering Department, foremost among which were the completion of the log books. Each engineer in charge of a watch carefully filled in the Engine Room 'Rough Log Book'. It was the Chief Engineer's duty to copy the entries from the 'Rough Log Book' into the Engine Room Log Book (the master copy) each day, as soon as possible after noon.

A repair book was provided in which were recorded all repairs to boilers, main and auxiliary machinery, tanks and hull, Board of Trade and other surveys, as well as the withdrawing of shafts and any tests of any kind that were carried out. The port and name of any contractors were also documented and the book retained for reference.

A fully detailed report of the condition of the ship was forwarded to the Superintendent Engineer twice yearly. This report included the state of the hull, decks, holds, bunkers, masts, funnels, stern frame, rudder, double bottoms, including floors and frames, passenger accommodation, refrigerating and electric light machinery, main engines, boilers and all auxiliaries.

The abstract of Engine Room Log Book, Stores Return and Water Return Forms were filled in by the Chief Engineer and forwarded to the Superintendent Engineer, along with the Engine Room Log Books, any indicator diagrams (giving an indication as to the main engines' indicated horsepower) that were taken at regular intervals during the voyage and other papers. He would also complete a Fuel Return form at the end of a voyage, which would be signed by the Captain and sent to Head Office.

The Chief Engineer would ensure that the Engineers' Storekeeper's Book was correctly kept and brought to him for examination each day at noon. In addition, he kept the Spare Gear and Tool Book himself in which he recorded all the articles received and expended. He had to make sure that all expenditures were replaced as soon as possible, especially spare gear. He would also ensure that all spare gear was the correct size for the working parts, and readily accessible, so that it could be fitted in the shortest possible time in an emergency. Spare gear that had become unsuitable owing to the wearing of the moving parts, and worn-out tools, were landed for adjustment or scrapping. The Assistant Superintendent Engineer responsible for repairs had to obtain authority from Head Office as to their disposal. A copy of the book was sent to the Superintendent Engineer's office each year and an inventory of all spare gear and tools was taken annually.

At the end of each voyage, the Chief Engineer had to send a detailed report to the Superintendent Engineer, which gave full particulars as to how the machinery had performed during the voyage. It included such things as whether it had been necessary to stop at any time and if so, for how long, on what dates and for what reason. If the cause of the stoppage was due to any neglect, to whom the neglect might be attributed, and what steps were taken to prevent a recurrence. He also had to give the reasons for any reduction in speed, or any material increase in fuel consumption and any reasons why the schedule time had not been kept. If any stores received during the voyage were unsatisfactory, the Chief Engineer was expected to submit full details and retain a sample to forward to the Superintendent Engineer's office if requested. He could send further reports during the voyage on the understanding that they did not interfere with the completeness of the Voyage Report.

Hydraulic machinery

The hydraulic machinery and all the spare gear were in the charge of the Chief Engineer, who was held responsible for their good keeping and efficient working order.

Refrigerating machinery and cold chambers

The Chief Engineer was responsible for keeping the refrigerating machinery in good condition and working order. He would arrange to run the machinery before the start of a voyage to allow sufficient time to reduce temperatures in the cold chambers.

Aspects of main engine operation

Before starting the main engines all the boilers would be raised to full steam and the main steam stop valves opened to the common supply steam main. The engine room bulkhead main steam stop valves would be open and steam made available up to the main regulating valve (or throttle). Oil pipes were proved clear by oil from a hand feeder. The links, link blocks, bell-cranks, Wyper shaft and drag links were oiled and run over to full travel in both directions by the hand reversing gear, after

BELOW One of the *Titanic*'s refrigerating engines that were situated on the port side of the reciprocating engine room. *(The Shipbuilder)*

which Brown's reversing gear was engaged. The cylinders were warmed through and heated by careful admission of steam through the valves by easing the regulating valve.

Drain cocks or valves, which were fitted to the top and bottom of each cylinder to remove the water of condensation from each end of the cylinder, were opened. The drains led to the auxiliary condenser.

When manoeuvring the engines the watch-keeping engineers would be at the centre of the bottom-most platform, known as the Starting Platform. This was located between the two main engines, adjacent to the forward LP cylinder columns. The main levers for engine operation were the direction lever, which operated the Brown's reversing engine, the regulating lever, the changeover valve operating lever and an adjacent panel of levers that controlled the drain cocks.

When entering or leaving port, the *Titanic's* Chief Engineer, along with two senior and three junior engineers, would take up station on the Starting Platform. The Chief Engineer's function was to oversee the safe, smooth and efficient operation of the Engine Room machinery while manoeuvring of the vessel was in progress. When the order came from the Bridge via the Engine Room telegraphs ringing (the first order before sailing was always 'Stand By'), a junior

RIGHT **Loud-speaking navy phones were fitted in the Chief Engineer's cabin, the engine room and stokeholds 1–6.** *(The Shipbuilder)*

engineer would answer the telegraphs by moving a handle to the requisite movement. Each movement was recorded by the third junior engineer in the Movements Book, along with each telegraph order and its time on the Engine Room clock. The two senior engineers operated the control levers on the Starting Platform, first by pulling over the direction lever for ahead or astern, which activated the Brown's reversing engine. The regulating valve lever was then operated, which allowed steam to enter the HP cylinder and piston valve; this was eased gently at first to turn over the engine and control the steam through the cylinders, and gradually pushed forward to speed up the engine. When manoeuvring was finished and the engines were under full away, the cylinder drain valves were shut after all the condensate had been blown out.

When coming towards the end of a passage and alongside or at anchor when the engines were no longer required, the last telegraph order was 'Stop'. As there was no 'Finished With Engines' order on the telegraphs this instruction was given verbally by the Officer of the Watch down the voice pipe to the manoeuvring platform.

The *Titanic's* marine engineers were drawn originally, with few exceptions, from time-served fitters and fitter-turners in Harland & Wolff's shipyard. After a sea-going period an engineer could progress up the Engine Room career structure by sitting exams for Board of Trade Second and First Class Certificates of Competency, and gaining watch-keeping experience at sea. Their principal function was to see the efficient and safe running of their boiler rooms and engine rooms along with their auxiliary machinery. They also ensured that the main power plant – along with any necessary lubrication and maintenance of running machinery – ran efficiently and without interruption.

Any large breakdown, such as a broken connecting rod or 'wiped' white metal bearing, could be repaired at sea with the requisite spare parts; larger breakdowns, like a cracked or sheared crankshaft or the shedding of a propeller blade, necessitated repairs by Harland & Wolff shore-side staff at Belfast or Southampton.

Steelwork repair and riveting

A common cause of damage to a vessel and its fittings was a collision, either by contact with jetties or exposed rocks, submerged hazards such as reefs, compacted ledges and banks, other vessels, or with movable (and thus unchartable) hazards such as derelicts, ships' wreckage, or ice.

In many of these instances the damage sustained was often caused to the fore part of the colliding ship's hull. Damage to plating could vary from slight indentation to being holed, with buckling or fracture to the associated plating and underlying supporting structure, such as the framing. Severe collisions could lead to the total loss of the ship.

At the time of the *Titanic* it was often necessary to dry-dock a ship to assess the damage and the extent of repairs required. Dry-docking was especially urgent if the damage lay beneath the waterline and involved the ingress of water into the watertight compartments, thus compromising the ship's stability and trim.

To dry-dock a ship a suitable dock was prepared, with dock blocks arranged to suit the keel line of the individual vessel and placed at a longitudinal angle if an excessive trim had been taken. Damaged plating was first removed by drilling out existing rivets. The rivets that edged the nearest sound, undamaged plate were drilled with care so that the existing rivet holes could be reused. This was done by punching an indentation mark (a 'centre pop') into the rivet head at its approximate centre and then using a drill of a lesser diameter than the underlying hole to drill down to the depth of the rivet head or countersunk. A backing-out punch was then applied, which, on the application of force, sheered the shank of the rivet away from the head and out through the other side of the plate(s), leaving the original hole more or less intact. If a rivet point had its shoulders faying (laying flatly together) with the parent plate, then the point could be chipped off before punching. Meanwhile, replacement plating was prepared.

The ship's framing, if not too severely affected, could sometimes be manually hammered back into alignment without the application of heat. If the structure had been badly buckled or fractured then the damaged frame(s) were removed by cleanly chipping the buckled lengths of frame away from the sound frame by using a 'windy hammer' – a hand-held pneumatic machine with a chipping

BELOW Two methods of cutting out rivets. *(Authors' Collections)*

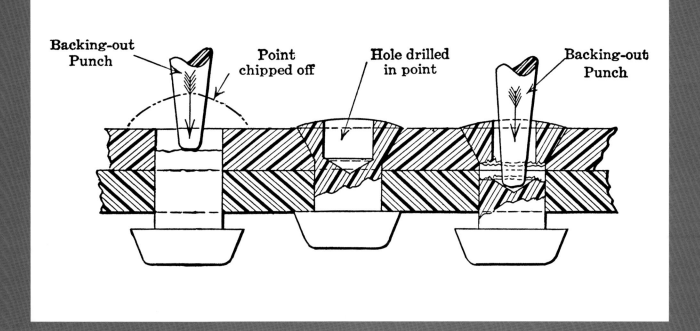

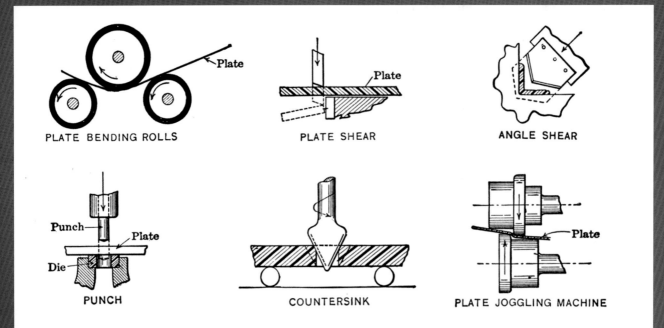

ABOVE Operation of shipyard machine tools. *(Authors' Collections)*

tool attached – a very noisy operation. The recently introduced method of oxy-acetylene burning might have been used, with care being taken that no flammable material was within the vicinity.

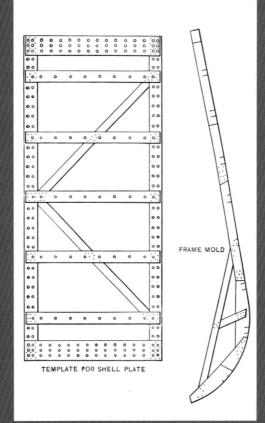

TEMPLATE FOR SHELL PLATE

FRAME MOLD

RIGHT Template for a shell plate and a mould for a frame – both made of strips of batten wood tacked together. *(Authors' Collections)*

Meanwhile, a replacement length of framing was prepared by using the body lines on the mould loft floor from which a template mould was prepared, normally using a length of steel rod bent to the correct shape. The moulding rod – or 'set iron' – was transferred to the Smiths' Shop where it was laid on a floor made up of 4in-thick steel bending slabs, and secured with metal dogs. The channel bar for the new frame was then made malleable in a furnace before being dragged to the bending slab where it was bent into shape against the mould either by hand using mauls, or by a portable frame-bending machine (Sir George Hunter developed such a machine which was used during the construction of the *Mauretania,* built at his yard on the River Tyne in 1906), or by a 'T'-shaped lever that had a pin at the angled junction of the shaft and curved cross-piece that slotted into a hole in the bending slab. On application to the shaft the lever turned about this pinion while the curved, crescent-shaped cross-bar of the 'T' acted as a cam to exert a bending force against the frame.

The new frame section could be made in one of two ways depending on how it was to be attached to the two cut ends of the original frame. In the first method, the new piece exactly matched the distance between the two cut ends left by the removal of the damaged frame, in which case butt straps were used to overlap the flanges of both original and new frames. These butts were double-riveted to the original frame where wide enough, with at least three rivets to each row and with an equal length of pre-drilled 'overhang' against which the new frame was attached.

The second method allowed for an extra length on each end of the replacement frame. This was of sufficient length to overlap the original cut ends (enough length being allowed for at least three rivets). The overlap could then be joggled – that is, bent by a joggling machine – into a narrow 'Z'-bend at the point of contact so that the overlap fayed (lay flatly together) against the ends of the original frame.

Before fitting, the replacement frames were drilled with holes of suitable diameters and spacings (such as six rivet diameters apart for watertight spacing) to take the rivets that attached the new plating to the hull. Once all replacement frames were in place a template (mould) could be made from deal moulding boards, 4in wide by 3/8in thick, the outer edges of which were erected at ship to reflect the outer edges of the replacement plate. Vertical boards were attached to coincide with the new frames and diagonal stiffening pieces were attached where required to enable the entire mould to retain its shape once lifted down from the hull.

While the mould/template remained bolted in place the locations of rivet holes were marked on to the wooden template from the holes in the new frames and from those existing in the surrounding plate edges. The rigid template was then transferred to the Plate Shop and laid on the replacement plate, the outline transferred and the hole positions marked.

The new plate could then be cut to size with any necessary shaping to suit local flair being applied in the rolling machine, and rivet holes being transferred from the wooden moulds to the plate which was then drilled or punched. The spacing of rivets was dictated by their position within the ship's structure. In areas that were not liable to contact with water (especially inside the vessel) the spacing was greater than in areas constantly exposed to the elements or even submerged. Spacings in compartments that contained oil were less than 'wet' areas.

Good alignment of holes and quality riveting was essential if rework was to be avoided. The aim of good riveting was to ensure that the head and hammered point of a rivet both lay symmetrically about the shank and that damage caused to the surrounding plate by hammering was avoided. Care had to be taken to ensure that holes were not too big for the rivet shanks, otherwise distortion to the latter would occur. Potential defects could be caused throughout the building process through faulty or careless workmanship from any of the trades concerned with marking-off, shaping and fitting a structural member, including loftsmen, smiths, bolters-up, mould-makers, shipwrights, drillers, reamers and riveters.

BELOW Portion of a bending slab, showing frame bending. *(Authors' Collections)*

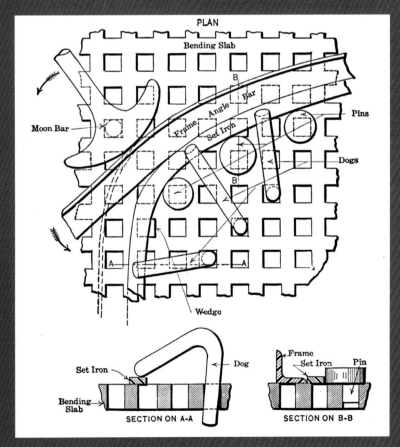

The *Titanic* Rediscovered

In July 1969 NASA's Apollo 11 landed men on the Moon, but up to that time technology was not ready or available to detect or locate the wreck of the *Titanic*.

For 73 years after the *Titanic* disappeared beneath the cold waters of the North Atlantic with a loss of 1,500 lives she remained lost in time to the world. But then in September 1985 her wreck, like some silent sentinel in a world of darkness, was disturbed when an expedition mounted by Dr Robert Ballard discovered the whereabouts of the *Titanic*'s remains 2½ miles down on the ocean floor.

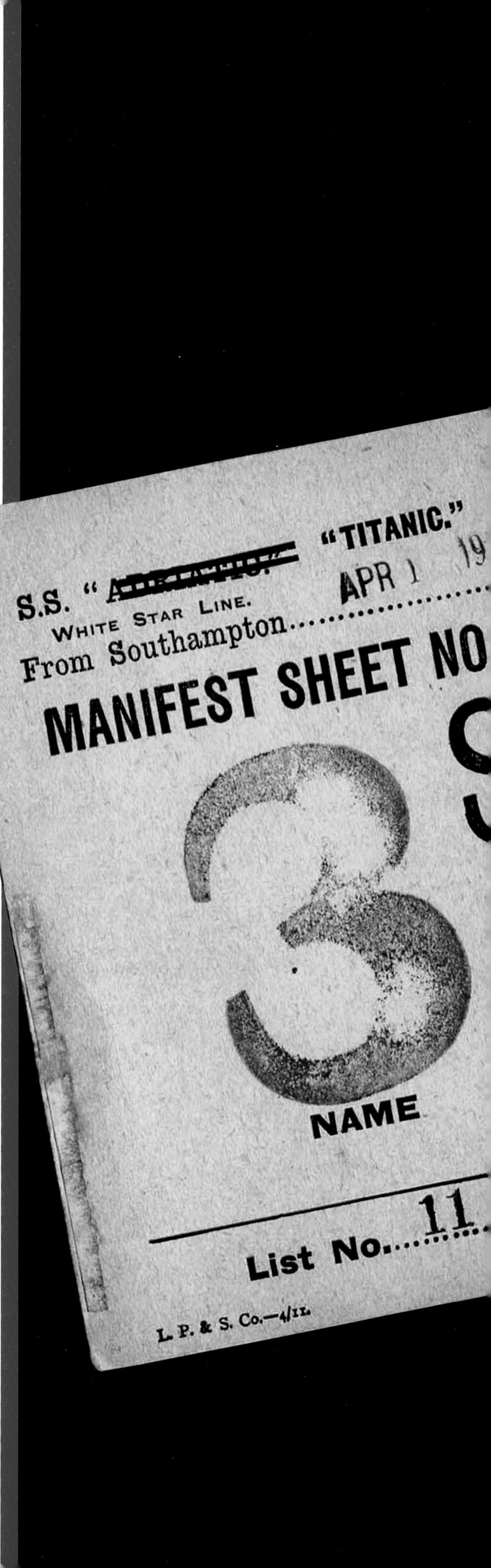

RIGHT *Titanic* **Third Class passenger inspection card.** *(TopFoto)*

S.S. "A̶̶̶̶̶̶" "TITANIC."
WHITE STAR LINE.   APR 1   19
From Southampton.........

MANIFEST SHEET NO

3

NAME

List No.......11

L. P. & S. Co.—4/12.

INSPECTION CARD

(Immigrants and Steerage Passengers).

Port of Departure, SOUTHAMPTON.

Date of Departure

No. of Contract.

342712

S.S. "~~ADRIATIC~~" "TITANIC," APR 10 1912

WHITE STAR LINE.

Name of Passenger, *Sarah Roth* ENGLAND.

Last Residence, ... Passed at quarantine, port of .... Passed by Immigration Bureau

Inspected and passed at
SOUTHAMPTON. .... U.S. port of ....

.... (Date)

(Date)

(The following to be filled in by ship's surgeon or agent prior to or after embarkation.)

No. on Ship's list or manifest.....11.....

S Ship's list or manifest........................

Berth No.   Steamship Inspection.   1st day   2   3   4   5   6   7   8   9   10   11   12   13   14   To be punched by ship's Surgeon at Daily Inspection.

M 721

**ABOVE A scene from James Cameron's film
Titanic, as the great liner begins its plunge to the
Atlantic seabed.** *(dpa-Film 20th Century Fox/DPA/
Press Association Images)*

The discovery of the wreck of the *Titanic*
helped unravel some of the mysteries and
unanswered questions of that fateful night of
14/15 April 1912.

There can be no doubt that the resurgence
of interest in the loss of the *Titanic* during
the latter part of the 20th century was initially
sparked by the late Walter Lord's book *A Night
to Remember*, in 1956, followed in 1958 by the
Rank Organisation film of the same title. The
film led to the second largest film set ever being
built at Pinewood Film Studios and the use of
the former Royal Mail liner *Asturias* for some
promenade deck and lifeboat lowering scenes.

Later, in 1963, the *Titanic* Historical Society
was established in the United States, and one
of its co-founders, William (Bill) H. Tantum IV,
was a fervent believer that one day the wreck
of the *Titanic* would be discovered. Bill Tantum,

**LEFT The bow of the *Titanic* looms out of the
darkness on the ocean floor, 12,500ft below the
surface of the North Atlantic.** *(AP Photo)*

a lifelong *Titanic* researcher and historian, had worked alongside diver and underwater explorer Jacques Cousteau in 1976 when they made a film for television, '*Calypso*'s Search for the *Britannic*'. For this Bill dived on the wreck of the *Britannic* (sunk in the First World War) in a small submersible from Cousteau's ship, the *Calypso*.

In 1977 Bill met Dr Robert Ballard of Woods Hole Oceanographic Institution of Woods Hole, Massachusetts, who had a shared vision of finding the wreck of the *Titanic*. By July 1980, a Texan entrepreneur and explorer, Jack Grimm, funded a scientific expedition which set out to locate the wreck, but the expedition was blighted by bad weather and equipment malfunction and they failed to locate it. A year later, in June 1981 and again in July 1983, further expeditions funded by Grimm proved unsuccessful. Then on 1 September 1985, a joint French and United States scientific expedition, led by Dr Ballard, finally discovered and photographed the remains of the *Titanic* at a depth of 12,460ft (2½ miles) on the ocean floor.

This expedition had been the realisation of 12 years of trying to raise funds to finance the venture, and convincing sceptics of the scientific and practical benefits of the project. They initially started their search with their vessel *Knorr* in a position between the *Titanic*'s last reported position and that of the vicinity where

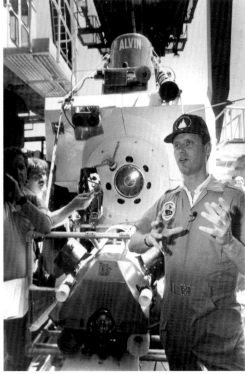

her lifeboats were recovered by the *Carpathia*. There followed a sonar search strategy (or sweep) by the French in which they spread their sonar sweep lines 2,600ft apart. The US effort took a more belt-and-braces approach whereby sonar was used in conjunction with a cable-fed submersible, *Argo*. This mounted a visual search strategy over the area. Because they were searching along any portion of roughly a mile of scattered debris, they operated along sweep lines 6,000ft apart. The *Argo* operated in 12,500ft depth of water, somewhat like an underwater kite. In the early hours of 1 September 1985, some wreckage was discovered, then one of the *Titanic*'s boilers. The next day the main hull was discovered upright.

The following year, in July 1986, Ballard returned to the wreck site with a second expedition. Diving in the submersible *Alvin*, and in conjunction with the remotely operated vessel *Jason Jr*, the entire wreck and debris field were explored, surveyed and photographed in greater detail, the submersible even landing on the *Titanic*'s deck. The expedition had confirmed that the wreck was in two large hull sections but on an even keel. The stern section was 1,970ft away from the main intact bow section, between was a debris field of artefacts and five scattered single-ended boilers from No. 1 Boiler Room and four cranes. It was Ballard's avowed intent that the wreck should remain undisturbed with nothing being removed from the site, a protocol about which he felt very strongly.

In 1987, Ballard's book *The Discovery of the Titanic* became an international number one best-seller, and was translated into eight languages. That year the US Congress moved

to make the *Titanic* an international memorial and a French expedition recovered some 900 artefacts from the sea bed and the wreck for George Tulloch's company RMS Titanic Inc. Many of these went on exhibition at the National Maritime Museum at Greenwich between October 1994 and April 1995.

In 1998, James Cameron's Oscar-winning epic movie *Titanic* was a block-buster in which a mock-up of the ship to seven-eighths scale was rebuilt, faithfully recreating detailed construction, artefacts and historical events of the disaster; albeit with the thread of a fictional onboard romance interweaving the actual story.

Appendix 1

Glossary

Afterbody The portion of the hull abaft the greatest transverse section, which is generally (but not always) the 'midship section', this being a datum of the hull of the ship.

Amidships (i) Used as a naval architectural term within the text of this manual, it means the midway point between the fore and after perpendiculars; (ii) As a seamanship term it is also used to describe anything lying in the line of the keel or the centre fore-and-aft line of the ship.

Beam (i) The greatest breadth measurement of a ship; (ii) Transverse structural member of a ship's framing, below the decks and supporting them against stresses, while checking racking tendencies in the transverse section.

Bearing Supports the heavy load or force of a moving or rotating component with minimum wear. (i) Plain journal bearing, used to support the weight of horizontal loads of rotating shafts, in which case the loads and forces are perpendicular to the shaft; (ii) Thrust bearing, used to resist and support axial loads and forces of rotating shafts, in which case the force is in a horizontal direction along the shaft.

Bilge Space where drain (bilge) water, residual oil, coal dust and ash collects at the bottom of the ship between the keel and the ribs (or frames) or at the sides of a double bottom.

Bilge keel A lesser keel, attached along the 'corners' of the hull externally, usually for 30–40% of the ship's length, to reduce rolling. A disadvantage is that it increases propulsive resistance by some 4%, and slightly more when the ship is pitching.

Boiler Used in a large vessel in which steam is raised from fresh water by the application of heat. In the *Titanic* the fire-tube or Scotch boiler had a series of furnaces connected with a common combustion chamber at the back of the boiler. To this combustion chamber were linked a series of tubes through which the gases generated in the furnace were passed. As they did so on their way to the funnel, they gave up their heat to water surrounding the fire tubes. (These boilers worked on the same principle as the old steam locomotives).

Bow The forward end of a ship.

Brass An alloy of copper (Cu) and zinc (Zn). When the proportions were 70% Cu, 30% Zn, this was often referred to as 'cartridge brass'. Used for castings, valves, tube plates and fittings that may be exposed to sea water.

Breadth (i) Extreme: The greatest measured breadth of a vessel, measured to the outside of the outside plating; (ii) Moulded: The greatest measured breadth of a vessel, measured inside the inner strakes of shell plating. Both these breadths generally occur amidships.

Bronze An alloy of copper (Cu) and tin (Sn).

Bulkhead A vertical partition (or wall), in a thwartship or fore-and-aft direction, which separates two compartments. These bulkheads were usually constructed of steel.

Bunker A compartment for storing fuel, whether coal or oil. Filling the bunkers with coal was normally referred to as 'coaling' or 'coaling ship'.

Cast iron An alloy of iron which contains 2–5% carbon, has compressive strength and the facility

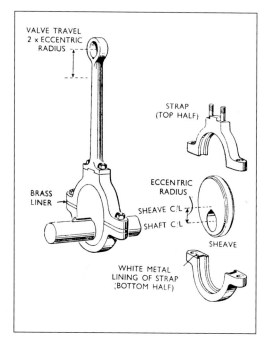

to be cast into intricate forms. In the marine steam engine, cast iron is used for the cylinders and covers, slide casings and valves, framing, plummer blocks, piston and condenser casing.

Caulking To make watertight, to seal. The caulking of steel plates is carried out with a pneumatic tool that makes a groove in the plate edge, the shoulder of the groove being forced against the adjacent plate.

Compartment An essential subdivision that provides a reasonable chance that the ship will remain afloat if it has been opened to the sea ('bilged'). *See also*: Watertight compartments.

Condenser A heat exchanger that converts steam back to water for further use in the boiler feed system. When the steam has done its work in the steam propulsion plant it passes into the condenser. This consists of nests of tubes through which cold sea water passes. Upon its impingement on the outside of these tubes, the steam condenses into water and is drawn off by the extraction pump. The act of condensation produces a vacuum, and in this manner steam pressure is applied at one end of the engine and suction is applied at the other, discharging the steam quickly and increasing the efficiency of the engine in terms of high pressure.

Counter stern Sometimes referred to as an 'overhanging stern'. In this type of stern (a hallmark of Harland & Wolff's construction), which generally accompanied the straight stem, the upper works extend beyond the rudder post, forming a continuation of the hull line. Generally half-round or elliptical in plan view, the counter stern needed to be framed so as to support its own weight as well as providing structural resistance to the battering of a following sea. The counter stern was, in effect, an extension of the hull above the stern post on which the rudder was hinged.

Davits Mechanisms for clearing and lowering (or hoisting) ships' lifeboats.

Deadweight A form of tonnage, which is in effect the carrying capacity of the ship. It is the difference between the lightweight and displacement tonnages, being the actual weight required to bring a vessel from her light draught to her loaded summer freeboard marks, and includes cargo, stores and fuel.

Dimensions All dimensions and data quoted are given, where known, in Imperial units (feet,

inches, tons) and not in SI Units. This has been done for two reasons: (i) The majority of particulars and measurements on the *Titanic* were originally documented in Imperial units and any conversion might lead to error or confusion; (ii) The Imperial system will be more familiar to the majority of English-speaking readers for the purposes of comparison and identification.

Draught extreme The distance measured from the waterline to the bottom of the keel, sometimes called the 'draught-bottom of keel'.

Draught moulded The distance measured from the waterline to the top of the keel.

Draw water A ship is said to 'draw' as much water as her maximum draught, which is generally rather more aft than forward. A ship must always have more water than her actual draught in which to proceed.

Dynamo Generally the rotating electrical element of a generator which produces direct current.

Eccentric Offset rotating motion where a component does not share a common centre as in concentric motion. Eccentric motion is used on steam reciprocating machinery to operate the piston or slide valve gear, which admits steam to the main pistons.

Eccentric strap The ring that is on the eccentric circumference to which an eccentric rod is attached.

Exchange rates *See* Monetary.

Expansion joints In the superstructure or deck plating, a sliding joint which permits linear

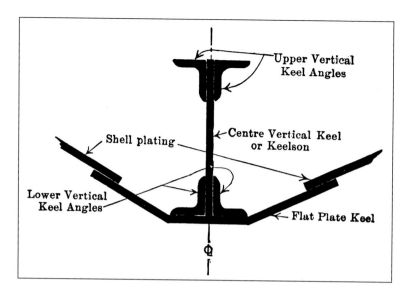

movement between adjacent sections when the ship is subjected to hogging and sagging stresses which might otherwise tend to be destructive.

Forebody The immersed body of the hull forward of the midship section, or point of maximum breadth.

Forefoot The lower part of the stem where it is stepped into the keel.

Freeboard The vertical distance between the waterline and the upper surface of the freeboard deck: that is, the upper deck having permanent means of closing all openings leading below.

Generator The unit that comprises a prime-mover (steam reciprocating engine) directly coupled to a dynamo which produces the electrical power in the ship.

Horsepower Power is the rate of doing work, and the horsepower was almost universally adopted as a rate for measuring work. The unit was devised by the engineer James Watt and was his estimate of the rate at which a good horse could work for a few hours, though he deliberately fixed it at a high amount. Concerning the *Titanic's* engines there are two basic types which should be considered: (i) Indicated horsepower (ihp) is the measured power per cylinder obtained from steam reciprocating engines and internal combustion engines. The horsepower is indicated by a small piece of equipment which records graphically (on an indicator diagram) the mean pressure in the cylinder at any position of the piston during its stroke. It is actually the horsepower indicated or developed by the engine at the time. (ii) Shaft horsepower (shp) is the measurement of output

of steam turbines and is the power transmitted by the machinery to the propellers. Shp is measured as close to the propellers as possible by means of one or more instruments known as 'torsion meters'. These measure the angle of twist caused in a known length of the shaft by the applied turning force, or torque.

Hull form The hull design, or shaping the underwater hull, so as to move the vessel through the water with a minimum of power wastage. It is desirable to combine hull form, propeller design and power to give the best results. Hull-form performance in the field of naval architecture was generally predicted from model tank testing.

Journal The main parts of the main crankshaft that are supported by bearings in the engine main frame.

Keel The keel, or flat plate keel as it is known when referring to steel-hulled vessels, is in reality the middle line strake of the outer bottom plating, and when considered in conjunction with the vertical keel and middle line strake of inner bottom plating, it forms a valuable longitudinal stiffener, or backbone, to the ship.

Knot All trials, service and cruising speeds are quoted in knots (kt). One knot is a velocity of one nautical mile per hour – a nautical mile being 6,080ft, which is the length of one minute of arc on the equator or of a meridian.

Length

Length Between Perpendiculars (lbp) The length measured in feet between a vertical line drawn through the intersection of the load waterline and the forward side of the stem (forward perpendicular/FP) and a line drawn perpendicular to the intersection of the after edge of the rudder post and the load waterline (after perpendicular/AP).

Length Overall (loa) The length in feet from the extreme forward point of the vessel to a similar point aft – i.e. the greatest measured length of the vessel.

Length/breadth ratio In wooden hulled ships the ratio of length to beam was about 7:1, sometimes less, the breadth being necessary for providing the required restoring action to counteract the overturning force of the wind against the sails. Many of the earlier Harland & Wolff steamships were made with a ratio of 10:1, and on occasion 11:1, thus increasing the relative payload. This contemporary practice became general for its steamships.

Manganese bronze An alloy of approximately 60% copper, 39% zinc and 1% ferro-manganese. It is much used for propeller blades and takes a fine polished surface, thus reducing friction. In some steam turbines the blades are often made of this alloy because of its high breaking stress.

Midship section The transverse section of the ship at amidships.

Monetary Any costs or fares to which reference is made in the text are usually in sterling or in US dollars. In the earlier part of the 20th century the approximate currency conversion was £1/$5.

Mould Loft A large wooden floor on which the ship's lines are drawn out to full size and 'faired'. The lines plan was normally marked in chalk.

Muntz metal A brass containing 60% Cu and 40% Zn. In marine work it is often used for condenser tubes and pump rods. It is non-corrosive in sea water and has about the same strength as wrought iron.

psi pounds per square inch (lb/in^2): The Imperial unit of pressure used when referring to the gauge working pressure of boilers, or absolute when dealing with sub-atmospheric pressure or vacuum.

Scantlings The thickness and dimensions of all rolled sections, plating, girders and other structural parts of a ship. Lloyd's, the classification society, lays down minimum scantlings, according to the type of vessel, to which the builders must adhere if the vessel is to obtain classification from the organisation.

Screws Screw propellers.

Scrieve Board A template or large portable board laid on the mould loft floor on which the finally faired body sections are 'scrieved' in with a knife. When complete, moulds taken from the boards are taken to the frame-bending shed as a pattern from which frames are bent or plates cut to size.

Sheer The longitudinal rise (usually curving) of the deck forward and aft from amidships.

Shell The outer hull (plating) of a ship.

Steam reciprocating machinery The oldest form of marine power transmission, which depends for its operation on the expansive working of steam. If steam is supplied under pressure to an enclosed vessel and allowed to expand, it will push against one of the walls in

doing so. If this wall is a piston inside a cylinder, then steam will act on the head of a piston, of which there are several in a row. These piston heads are connected to piston rods that pass through steam-tight flanges at the bottom of the cylinders and go down to where they are connected via rods to the propeller shaft, known at this point as the crankshaft. As the steam passes from cylinder to cylinder, it repeats this movement, each piston being bigger than the preceding one because the steam, being weaker, works at a lower pressure and more of it is required to force down the piston head.

Steam turbines These are somewhat similar in operation to a windmill, with steam taking the place of the wind as a driving force, and with the utilisation of many vanes, known as 'blades', instead of the large sails of the windmill. A series of wheels, with their numerous blades, are mounted on a shaft in a steam-tight casing. In the case of the *Titanic*, the exhaust steam from the two sets of reciprocating engines enters the casing with force, impinges on the blades and turns the wheels. The rotating movement is directly transferred to the propeller shaft.

Steel A generic term for all compounds of iron and carbon where the latter does not exceed 1.5%. When the percentage of carbon is below 0.5% the material is more commonly known as mild steel. Steel is used in its rolled form for bars, plates, frames, girders and rivets in the

BELOW *The Titanic's* **engine room floods as the hull is split open by the iceberg. From the film *A Night to Remember*.** *(Authors' Collections)*

ship construction process. In the forged form it is used for main engine forgings such as pistons and connecting rods, valve rods and eccentric rods, all studs and bolts, shafting and turbine rotors.

Strake Any particular range of plates, abutting each other and of approximately the same width, running fore and aft along the length of the ship.

Strength Deck Generally, all decks contribute to the strength of a ship, but the uppermost one (sometimes called the Shelter Deck), which offers resistance to longitudinal bending, is the Strength Deck. It is thicker than the other decks at the line of hull, to withstand bending forces due to the ship's motion, and is slightly cambered, thereby also providing additional strength to support deck loads.

Superstructure The structure or deck houses built upon the hull. On passenger ships, the superstructure rises in tiers of promenade and other decks, and includes the Bridge, small houses and sometimes numerous ventilators and other fittings.

Telemotor A remote control device that assists in the operation of steering gear.

Tonnage

Displacement tonnage A measure of the amount (mass) of water displaced by a ship floating at a particular draught, equivalent to the weight of the ship. The displacement, expressed in tons, may be calculated by consideration of the underwater dimensions of the ship (length, breadth and draught) in conjunction with a figure for the vessel's block coefficient. The size of warships is normally expressed in displacement tonnage, but it is used in connection with merchant vessels, particularly passenger ships, in their design stages. Denoted as Δ^t.

Gross tonnage Defined as a measure of the under-deck tonnage with the addition of 'tween deck spaces and other enclosed spaces above the upper deck. Certain spaces are exempt from measurement. The size of many merchant ships is quoted in gross tonnage (particularly passenger ships), where the ton is $100ft^3$ volume. Denoted as gt.

Watertight compartments These are formed by steel watertight bulkheads (walls) built across the ship at certain sections. When the principal vertical bulkheads do not terminate at a watertight deck, their upper edges should be carried to a sufficient height above the waterline to prevent the water in a breached compartment flowing over the tops of the bulkheads into the adjoining compartments, even when the ship is deeply immersed due to the compartments being full of water.

White metal Used as a bearing material, usually melted and tinned on to brass or sometimes as dovetailed white metal strips. At the time of the *Titanic* the following alloying constituents were found to be ideal for bearings carrying a heavy load: 87% Sn, 5% Cu and 8% antimony. Slight variations from these exact proportions may be made by using 2–7% copper, the tin being adjusted accordingly. The alloy has a melting point of around 600°F so that when a bearing overheats it is apt to run out or 'wipe'. Such bearings require careful lubrication and watching.

Wrought iron Pure iron free from carbon and other impurities. The cast billet would be steam-hammered into shape and passed through a rolling mill. Used in the manufacture of anchor chains and rivets.

Appendix 2

Where *Titanic*-related artefacts can be seen

GENERAL

Titanic: The Artifact Exhibition
www.rmstitanic.net
This travelling exhibition created by RMS Titanic, Inc, showcases more than 300 artefacts recovered from Titanic's debris field. Venues in the USA, Canada, the UK and Australia.

UNITED KINGDOM

Merseyside Maritime Museum
www.liverpoolmuseums.org.uk
Titanic, Lusitania and the Forgotten Empress gallery.
Merseyside Maritime Museum, Albert Dock,
Liverpool L3 4AQ.

Southampton Maritime Museum
www.southampton.gov.uk
Permanent exhibition that tells the story of Titanic's crew.
The Wool House, Town Quay Road,
Southampton SO14 2AR.

Ulster Folk and Transport Museum
www.nmni.com/uftm
Permanent exhibition focusing on the construction, loss and legend of the Titanic.
Ulster Folk & Transport Museum, Cultra, Holywood, Co.
Down BT18 0EU, Northern Ireland.

The White Swan Hotel, Alnwick, Northumberland
www.classiclodges.co.uk/
The_White_Swan_Hotel_Alnwick
The White Swan is probably best known for its Olympic Dining Suite, which features the magnificent panelling, mirrors and stained glass windows from the Titanic's sister ship.
The White Swan, Bondgate Within,
Alnwick, Northumberland, NE66 1TD

UNITED STATES

Titanic Museum Attraction – Branson, Missouri
www.titanicbranson.com
'The World's Largest Titanic Museum Attraction' is a half-scale Titanic replica featuring 400 artefacts.
3235 76 Country Blvd & Hwy 165,
Branson, MO, USA.

Titanic Museum Attraction – Pigeon Forge, Tennessee
www.titanicpigeonforge.com
Run by the same company as the one in Branson, it also claims to be 'The World's Largest Titanic Museum Attraction'.
2134 Parkway, Pigeon Forge, TN 37863, USA.

The Titanic Museum – Indian Orchard, Massachusetts
www.titanic1.org
Maintained by the Titanic Historical Society, this small museum contains original blueprints donated by the builders of the Titanic, the life-jacket of Titanic's wealthiest and most famous passenger, John Jacob Astor, and the original wireless message that never made it to the bridge of the Titanic.
208 Main Street,
Indian Orchard, MA 01151-0053, USA.

Titanic The Experience – Orlando, Florida
www.titanictheexperience.com
This exhibit contains over 200 artefacts as well as full-scale recreations of the Titanic's Grand Staircase, First Class Parlour Suite, Boilers, and Promenade Deck.
7324 International Drive, Orlando, FL 32819, USA.

CANADA

Maritime Museum of the Atlantic – Halifax, Nova Scotia
www.museum.gov.ns.ca
Halifax was the closest major port to the site of the Titanic sinking and many of the recovered bodies and pieces of wreckage were transferred there. The Titanic exhibit at the Maritime Museum of the Atlantic features some of the wooden items retrieved from the water, including a nearly perfectly preserved deckchair.
1675 Lower Water Street,
Halifax, Nova Scotia, Canada B3J 1S3.

East Hants Historical Society – Maitland, Nova Scotia
www.ehhs.weebly.com
The East Hants Historical Society Museum in Maitland, Nova Scotia, is where you can see the table that was used to embalm John Jacob Astor.
East Hants Historical Museum, #6971, Rte 215,
Lower Selma, Nova Scotia, Canada.

Appendix 3

Useful Titanic-related contacts

WEBSITES

encyclopedia-titanica
www.encyclopedia-titanica.org
RMS Titanic facts and history.

Titanic-Titanic.com
www.titanic-titanic.com
One of the largest Titanic information resources on the Internet.

Titanic Inquiry Project
www.titanicinquiry.org
Transcriptions of the entire texts of the Senate and the British Titanic Inquiries.

Titanic – The Ship Magnificent
www.titanic-theshipmagnificent.com
Detailed examination of the ship's construction and fittings.

RMS Titanic, Inc
www.rmstitanic.net
RMS Titanic, Inc is the only company permitted by law to recover objects from the wreck site of Titanic. Since 1994 it has conducted seven research and recovery expeditions to Titanic's debris field and recovered more than 5,500 artefacts.

Expedition Titanic
www.expeditiontitanic.com
Virtual tour of the Titanic wreck.

TITANIC SOCIETIES

Belfast Titanic Society
www.belfast-titanic.com
32 Heatherstone Road,
Bangor, Co. Down BT19 6AE,
Northern Ireland.

British Titanic Society
www.britishtitanicsociety.com
British Titanic Society,
PO Box 401,
Hope Carr Way, Leigh,
Lancs WN7 3BB.

Canadian Titanic Society
www.canadian-titanic-society.com
Site 25-73,
Simcoe, Ontario N3Y 5K7,
Canada.

Scandinavian Titanic Society
www.scandtitanic.com
Box 2011,
SE-103 11 Stockholm,
Sweden.

Swiss Titanic Society
www.titanicverein.ch
Titanic-Verein Schweiz,
Postfach 8152 Glattbrugg,
Switzerland.

The Irish Titanic Society
www.iths.ie
Irish Titanic Historical Society,
4 Fancourt Road,
Balbriggan, Co Dublin,
Ireland.

The Titanic Historical Society Inc
www.titanichistoricalsociety.org
The Titanic Museum,
208 Main Street, Indian Orchard,
Massachusetts, USA.

Titanic International Society
titanicinternationalsociety.org
PO Box 416,
Midland Park, NJ 07342-0416,
USA.

Bibliography

Admiralty, *Naval Marine Engineering Practice Vol. I – BR 3003 (1)* (HMSO, 1959)

Ballard, Dr Robert D., *The Discovery of the Titanic* (Hodder & Stoughton Ltd, 1989)

Bell, James I., *Every Man His Own Shipwright* (Chantry Publications Ltd, 1950)

Blake, Harold S., *The Lifeboat: Its Construction, Equipment and Management* (Brown, Son & Ferguson Ltd, 1933)

Blocksidge, Ernest W., *Ship's Boats* (Longmans, Green and Co., 1920)

Carmichael, A.W., *Practical Ship Production* (McGraw-Hill, 1941)

Daish, H., Forrest, J., Sword, J., and Embleton, W., *Reed's Engineering for Masters, Mates and Junior Engineers* (Thomas Reed & Co. Ltd, n.d.)

Davey & Co., *Catalogue 10/61* (Davey & Co, n.d.)

de Haan, Ing. J.P., *Practical Shipbuilding – Rigging, Equipment and Outfit of Seagoing Ships, Volume IIIB, Part 1* (The Technical Publishing Company H. Stam, Haarlem, Holland, 1957)

Fisher, W.A., *Engineering for Nautical Students* (Brown, Son & Ferguson Ltd, 1936)

Frost, Ted, *From Tree to Sea* (Terence Dalton, 1985)

Gaasbeek, Richard Montgomery Van, *A Practical Course in Wooden Boat and Ship Building* (Frederick J. Drake & Co., 1919)

Garyantes, H.F., *Handbook for Shipwrights* (McGraw-Hill, 1941)

Haldane, J.W.C., *Steamships and Their Machinery from First to Last* (E. & F.N. Spon, London. 1893)

Hardy, A.C., *From Slip to Sea* (James Brown & Son (Glasgow) Ltd., 1926)

Horsnaill, W.O., *Understanding Marine Engines by Q & A* (English Universities Press, 1943)

Hutchings, David F., *The Titanic Story* (The History Press, 2008)

Hutchings, David, *Titanic – A Modern Legend* (Kingfisher Railway Productions, 2004)

de Kerbrech, Richard, *Ships of the White Star Line* (Ian Allan, 2009)

Lagan Boat Company, *Thomas Andrews' Notebook* (Lagan Boat Company, 1913; facsimile c.2008)

Layton, C.W.T., *Ship's Lifeboats – A Handbook for the Ministry of Transport Examination for Certificates in Lifeboat Efficiency, 2nd Ed* (Brown, Son & Ferguson, 1948)

Leather, John, *Clinker Boatbuilding* (Adlard Coles, 1987)

Lightoller, Commander, *Titanic and Other Ships* (Bay Tree Book)

Liversidge, John G., *Engine Room Practice – A Handbook for the Royal Navy & Mercantile Marine* (Charles Griffin & Co., 1911)

Lloyd's Register of Shipping, *Anchors – Approved Designs* (October 1945)

MacGibbon, W.C., Martin, A., and Barr, H., *B.o.T. Orals and Marine Engineering Knowledge, 6th Ed* (James Munro & Co Ltd, n.d.)

McCarty, Jennifer Hooper & Foecke, Tim, *What Really Sank the Titanic* (Citadel Press, 2008)

McCluskie, Tom, *Anatomy of the Titanic* (PRC Publishing, 1998)

Miller, S.W., *Oxy-Acetylene Welding* (The Industrial Press, New York, 1916)

Newnes Marine Engineering Data Sheets (Newnes, c.1954)

Nicol, George, *Ship Construction and Calculations, 6th Ed* (Brown, Son & Ferguson Ltd, 1937)

PRO Publications, *Facsimile No. 226 of 300 of 'Report on the Loss of the "Titanic" (S.S.)* (The National Archives/Public Record Office)

Ramsay, R.J., *Paddle Steamer Machinery – A Layman's Guide* (PSPS, 2000)

Seaton, A.E., *A Manual of Marine Engineering* (Charles Griffin & Co., 1907)

Sennett, R., and Oram, H.J., *The Marine Steam Engine* (Longmans & Co., 1898)

Sothern, J.M.W., *'Verbal' Notes and Sketches for Marine Engineer Officers,* 11th Ed (Crosby, Lockwood & Son, 1924)

Stansbie, J.H., *Iron and Steel* (Archibald Constable & Co. Ltd, 1907)

The Institute of Marine Engineers, *The Running and Maintenance of Marine Machinery* (Institute of Marine Engineers, 1965)

The Ocean Liners of the Past: Olympic & Titanic (The Shipbuilder/Patrick Stephens, 1976)

Thearle, Samuel J.P., *The Modern Practice of Shipbuilding in Iron and Steel (Volume I: Text & Volume II: Plates)* (William Collins, 1886 and 1902)

Thearle, Samuel J.P., *Theoretical Naval Architecture (Volume I: Text & Volume II: Plates)* (William Collins, 1889)

Thirkell, C.H., and Staff of Bennett College, *Marine Engineering* (The Bennett College, Sheffield, n.d.)

Tod and McGibbon, *B.o.T. Question and Answers for Marine Engineers* (James Munro & Co. Ltd, 1917 and 1918)

Way, R. Barnard, and Green, Noel D., *The Modern Ship* (Wells Gardner, Darton & Co., c.1939)

Various anon, *Great Industries of Great Britain* (circa.1880)

Walton, T. & Baird J., *Steel Ships – Their Construction and Maintenance,* 8th Ed (1944)

Williams, David L., and de Kerbrech, Richard, *Damned by Destiny* (Teredo Books Ltd, 1982)

Lecture notes and technical papers

Braunschweiger, Art, *Titanic's Engine Rooms, Parts 1 & 2* (Titanic Research & Modelling Association, February 2006, March 2006)

Halpern, Samuel, *Titanic's Prime Mover – An Examination of Propulsion and Power* (Encyclopedia-Titanica, 2007)

Hutchings, David, *Admiralty Trade Notes for Shipwright Apprentices* (HM Royal Dockyard, Portsmouth, 1961–66)

Newman, Brian, *Research Monograph No 3: Materials Handling in British Shipbuilding 1850–1945* (The Centre for Business History in Scotland, 1996)

Newman, Brian, *Research Papers in the History of British Shipbuilding, No 1: Plate and Section Working Machinery in British Shipbuilding 1850–1945* (Centre for Business History in Scotland, July 1993)

South Shields Marine & Technical College, *Correspondence Course for Marine Engineer Cadets* (1963–1965)

Welin, Axel, *The Arrangement of Boat Installations of Modern Ships* (53rd Session of the Institution of Naval Architects, 29 March 1912)

Index